Cotton

Cotton

Companies, Fashion & The Fabric of Our Lives

Joseph H. Hancock, II, Nioka N. Wyatt & Tasha L. Lewis

intellect Bristol, UK / Chicago, USA

First published in the UK in 2016 by
Intellect, The Mill, Parnall Road, Fishponds, Bristol, BS16 3JG, UK

First published in the USA in 2016 by
Intellect, The University of Chicago Press, 1427 E. 60th Street, Chicago,
IL 60637, USA

A catalogue record for this book is available from the
British Library.

Cover images are courtesy of Raleigh Denim

Cover designer and typesetting: Holly Rose and Emily Dann
Production manager: Matthew Floyd
Copy-editors: Nissa Lee and Emma Rhys
Dr. Joseph H. Hancock, II's back cover photo is courtesy of Dennis J. Photography, New York.

ISBN 978-1-78320-685-8
ePDF ISBN 978-1-78320-686-5
ePUB ISBN 978-1-78320-687-2

Printed & bound by Gomer Press Ltd, UK

The Authors Dedicate This Book To Their Families, Friends and Students Who Inspire Us Each Day

Contents

Acknowledgements

Joseph H. Hancock, II
Nioka N. Wyatt
Tasha L. Lewis

Well they said it couldn't be done… There is no way you can produce a book using just undergraduate and graduate students that would be academically sound and make a significant contribution to the fashion, clothing, textiles and business disciplines body of academic research. But with the generous help of Cotton University, funding for *Cotton: Companies, Fashion and the Fabric of Our Lives* was awarded in whole through a competitive grant presented to Joseph H. Hancock, II, Nioka N. Wyatt and Tasha L. Lewis by the Importer Support Program of the Cotton Board and Cotton Incorporated; and through their generosity and by being a proud supporter of our grant we were able to produce this wonderfully illustrated book. *We did it!*

This was a great team of scholars, students and editors who rolled-up their sleeves and got to work in order to create a top-notch publication, demonstrating the interdisciplinary nature of our disciplines and the teamwork that can be created when three major universities decide to work together in order to do high quality experiential research for academe. We had a great time with a few bumps in the road, and we have managed to create a book that demonstrates the integrity of the cotton industry, the evolution of fashion design, and recalls the importance of manufacturing high quality products that can be enjoyed by consumers for years… instead of just a few months.

We hope that you enjoy this book and that it motivates many readers to continue investigations into the world of cotton and how it became *the fabric of our lives*.

Joseph H. Hancock, II
This book would not have existed without the support of many individuals who helped to make it possible. First, I would like to thank Cotton University for their funding and substantial support of this project. I hope they continue their educational programming that serves many of our students around the globe. Next, I want to personally thank Intellect who produced this wonderful book, especially Jessica Mitchell, James Campbell, Bethan Ball and Emily Dann. A special *thank you* for all your time goes to Matthew Floyd, who was very patient with this team in the production of the book. He deserves a raise! In addition, thanks are deserved for the book's copy-editors Nissa Lee and Emma Rhys. I would like to thank Drexel University, Antoinette Westphal College of Media Arts & Design, the Robert and Penny Fox Historic Costume Collection, the Drexel University Custom-Design Major and the Department of Design for all their support. A special thank you goes to my two students Virginia Theerman from Design & Merchandising and Stevie Guarino from the Custom-Design Major for their thorough investigations and chapters in this book… I hope they are

pleased with the outcome, as they should be! I would also like to personally thank Raleigh Denim and the Robert and Penny Fox Historic Costume Collection that opened their doors to allow my students to conduct their research projects and write such lovely chapters.

I would like to recognize my co-editors Nioka N. Wyatt and Tasha L. Lewis who did a fantastic job with this book and who put up with me through the entire process. They are very special to me and I consider them very good friends. Philadelphia University and Cornell University are very lucky to have two such wonderful educators and scholars. To my very special friends and colleagues, Patricia Cunningham, Joy Sperling, Patricia Giannelli, Clare Sauro, Kevin Egan, Alphonso McClendon, Anne Cecil, Beth Phillips, Nick Cassway, Kristen Ainscoe, Jill Lusen, Marie Graham, Danny and Kathy Bailey, Bill and Marianne Doyle, Gordon and Pam Comrie, Lee Halper, Reuben Wouch, Anthony Maitoza, Roberta Gruber and Allen Sabinson… I appreciate you putting up with my ramblings about fashion scholarship. Most importantly, thanks go to the three most important people in my life who live with me day-in and day-out, my life partner Edward A. Augustyn, my mother Margaret 'Peggy' Miller and our dog Ruby. These three really endure all the rigours of writing and publishing along with me and I love them for it!

Nioka N. Wyatt
It was a great opportunity to work with an ensemble of people who believed in the value of this book, evoked the spirit of collaboration and creative storytelling, while having fun along the way. I would like to extend my deepest appreciation to the companies that supported the book project, conducted tours and were extremely gracious with sharing information. The time you shared with the team to discuss your holistic experiences throughout the supply chain of fashion enhanced my methods of teaching and creative thinking. To the team below and the people who continue to support my dreams. Many thanks to Philip Spector, Stephanie Nawrocki, Claire Hach and Mary Murphy at Fashions Unlimited; Linda Iem, Senior Technical Designer at Lilly Pulitzer and Ashley Silbernagel, Product Development and Production Supervisor at Lilly Pulitzer; Alicia Pinckney, alumna of Philadelphia University; Mark Sunderland, Teri Loftus, Robert Skomorucha

and Keri Rapp at Philadelphia University; Boqian Wang and Brooke Wimberley for editing the images – students at Philadelphia University; and the Henry Cotton Retail Establishment in Venice, Italy. And my deepest gratitude goes to the team at Cotton Incorporated for supporting faculty development and allowing us to use their platform to extend our knowledge in all things cotton.

Tasha L. Lewis
The experience of working on this project was rewarding and truly an opportunity to showcase the talents of all of those involved. The evolving nature of the domestic fashion industry, particularly manufacturing, is a story that has many facets.

I would like to express my sincere gratitude to Cotton Incorporated for enabling us to present a compelling profile of the current state of domestic manufacturing. I am impressed with the outcome of this collaboration and exceedingly thankful for the opportunity to work with colleagues, students and industry innovators. I would like to thank my dream-team of students – Autumn, Helen and Sarah – for their outstanding contributions and commitment to this project. I am also extremely grateful to the people and companies that shared their stories and spaces with us: Grace Gouin and Mariano DeGuzman at Appalatch; Susan Barton, Megan Meikeljohn, Shona Barton Quinn and Claire Whitecomb at Eileen Fisher; and Tara St James at STUDY NY.

Cotton Incorporated is a research and promotion organization representing America's cotton producers and importers. The company's mission is to increase the demand and profitability of cotton through a range of research and marketing activities focused on the entire supply chain, from the farm all the way to the end consumer. The company likes to say that the consumer is engaged 'from dirt to shirt'. Cotton Incorporated has research programmes in agriculture, sustainability and textiles as well as marketing programmes targeted to mills, brands, retailers and consumers. Through all of these programmes, it supports the industry by communicating the value proposition of cotton and cotton products through an extensive range of services and product development opportunities.

At the farm level, Cotton Incorporated helps growers increase yield while decreasing inputs and lowering production costs. Through agricultural research, it promotes technology that leads to improved profitability and decreased impact on the environment. Many of the company's efforts target improvements in fibre quality, keeping cotton both a competitive fibre and one that is responsibly produced.

Cotton Incorporated focuses the majority of its research and development on apparel, home products and nonwovens. The organization develops new and improved products to advance cotton's position in the retail marketplace. Decisions about which products to explore are determined by market analysis, consumer needs and trend forecasts. The fashion-trend team travels the globe analysing the latest trends in colours, fabrications and silhouette. These trend experts provide direction to the global textile supply-chain network, which is committed to integrating cotton in their product offering.

In Cotton Incorporated's state-of-the-art research facility in Cary, North Carolina, scientists and engineers are able to research the most pressing issues in textiles, technology, trends and consumer science. Beginning with fibre processing, the yarn manufacturing facility conducts research and runs trials that address important manufacturing needs and issues. The research centre has the same capabilities as most modern vertical textile mills, and Cotton Incorporated researchers often work collaboratively with university and industry partners to enhance the knowledge and sustainability of cotton. *Cotton: Companies, Fashion & The Fabric of Our Lives* was funded by a grant from Cotton Incorporated. The Cotton Student Sponsorship Program provides support to select programmes at universities and colleges for the purpose of advancing the awareness and use of cotton among college and university students. Cotton Incorporated, under the Importer Support Program, administers the programme for Cotton Research.

As part of the ongoing effort to create new and innovative fabric ideas, researchers developed 100 per cent cotton and cotton-rich fabrications in the product development laboratory. A team of designers and engineers developed fabric collections called FABRICAST™, which offer the industry innovative and

Left hand page: Figure 1: Cotton field in Lubbock, Texas, home to the Plains Cotton Cooperative Association. (Photo by Emma Sidoriak.)

Figure 2: Cotton plant. (Photo by Jessica Zuzack.)

Figure 3: Students touring the spinning department at Cotton Incorporated headquarters. (Photo by Nioka N. Wyatt.)

Figure 4: Student viewing samples of innovative cotton fabrics at Cotton Incorporated headquarters. (Photo by Nioka N. Wyatt.)

creative options for cotton fabric concepts. The technical applications provided to customers include all the information necessary to produce the fabrics.

Cotton Incorporated also explores the areas of preparation, dyeing, finishing and printing. The technical experts are constantly researching new finishes and ways to improve efficiencies by reducing water, energy and chemical inputs. An innovative laboratory is equipped to research unique applications and finishing techniques in digital printing. The facility also has a state-of-the-art testing laboratory for fibres and material applications.

Cotton Incorporated conducts technical education workshops to help retailers and brands better meet consumer expectations. These workshops are funded and managed by the Importer Support Program of Cotton Incorporated and the Cotton Board. Lilly Pulitzer is one of the companies featured in the book and supports its staff by allowing the team to attend the seminars, workshops and other special events that will enhance the technical skills of their employees. Nioka N. Wyatt, associate professor at Philadelphia University, also mentioned that the training and knowledge she gained from attending the seminars while working at the home-shopping mogul QVC (Quality, Value, Convenience) allowed her to foster her career in academia and diversify her skills in teaching courses in material development, quality assurance and business development.

The online educational institution, Cotton University™, has everything you need to know about cotton from the latest trends to specific technical developments to a variety of self-paced online textile courses. The site also highlights career trajectories in the fashion industry with leading executives at Under Armour, Saks Fifth Avenue, Phillips-Van Heusen (PVH), Kohl's, and many other companies. The career snapshots are a great resource for students and industry representatives to gain insight into the role of trend forecasting with Linda DeFranco at Cotton Incorporated. There is also a vast online community, where you can network, start groups, post questions and share ideas about cotton and cotton textiles on a global scale. A series of contests, innovative marketing strategies and highlights from Cotton's 24-Hour Runway Show are featured on the site. In 2012, Alicia Pinckney – a former student at Philadelphia University who is currently studying in Milan, Italy – was a winner in the Cotton 24-Hour Runway Show. She received an all-inclusive ticket to Miami, Florida, to showcase her men's collection.

Cotton Incorporated provides additional services such as fibre economics and market research to help identify and analyse trends that affect cotton markets in the United States and globally. The 'Monthly Economic Letter' provides updates on US and world cotton information with analysis of the latest key statistics. Through consumer market research, Cotton Incorporated provides in-depth insights that focus on important industry and consumer trends. A wealth of information is provided to industry to make the appropriate decisions for their businesses.

Figure 5: Denim designs developed at Cotton Incorporated headquarters. (Photo by Nioka N. Wyatt.)

The research and information services are distributed to the entire textile industry in a variety of ways, from published research reports and technical bulletins to technical service trips, during which their experts meet and advise textile suppliers around the world. A dedicated team of marketing account managers works directly with manufacturers, brands and retailers to provide the information they need to enhance their cotton business. Through advertising, public relations, fashion marketing and retail promotions, Cotton Incorporated increases the interest of consumers through multiple media platforms. Cotton Incorporated has collaborated with MTV and vocalists to share how cotton has impacted their lives, through commercials with music artists like Jasmine Sullivan from Philadelphia.

Cotton Incorporated is an organization that supports fashion companies; embodies cotton innovation; and strives to support students, faculty and the global community. Because it is a not-for-profit organization funded by US growers of upland cotton and importers of cotton goods, the majority of its services are free of charge to those in the industry who use cotton. No matter where your business falls in the cotton supply chain, no matter what challenges you face, Cotton Incorporated is a resource partner that can support your future cotton projects. Please visit www.cottonuniversity. org or www.cottoninc.com for the most recent news, materials and developments in cotton research and innovation.

Cotton has long been a presence in the human experience, as a fibre, yarn, textile, garment, and in many, many other permutations. This article gives a brief historical overview of highlights in the history of cotton, with an emphasis on the relationship between cotton, costume history and the United States. Spanning from pre-history and the development of cotton in India to the present day and Cotton Incorporated, this article provides a broad-view story of the world's most familiar fibre.

Introduction

When researching the history of cotton, it is nearly impossible to separate the historical thread of the cotton fibre from the history of humanity itself. To write about cotton is to write about a plant, a textile, manufacturing, technology, labour, advertising, medicine, economics, date night, family values, beach towels and everything in between. Quite simply, cotton has impacted every touch point of the human experience. From an awkward T-shirt commemorating an event, to the ridiculously patterned drapes in a new restaurant, to the adorable blue and pink striped cotton blanket swaddling a newborn, cotton is everywhere. Cotton's ubiquity makes it commonplace, and yet it has been used to create magnificent works of art, luxurious surroundings, and even denote high socio-economic standing. The simplest of fibres, both ancient in use and modern in function, captures the essence of the human experience in every strand.

It is important to note that this history of cotton will primarily examine the fibre as it relates to western life and fashions both high and low. Cotton has a far-reaching global impact; books about the impact of cotton in just one country over time could easily number in the dozens. The work of processing the fibre from plant growth to final product has inspired volumes and volumes of scholarly literature. Think of this history as an anecdotal one, where context is given with a broad brush, enough to paint in those few outlines with particular interest, but by no means comprehensive.

Cotton from pre-history to global exploration

Cotton has wavered from a luxury good to the commonest of materials, sometimes playing a leading role in the global market, other times hanging back as it was overwhelmed by the popularity of silk from the East or by the production of rayon and other synthetic fibres popularized post-World War II. Yet it has always been present in some form, since its humble beginnings in the ancient days of early civilizations. Cotton rose out of the Indus River Valley in what is now modern India sometime around 2,000 BCE (Lemire [1987] 2013: 11). Evidence of a more advanced and organized cotton industry in India dates back to approximately 800 BCE, and as trade developed between India and the surrounding countries, cotton spread throughout the island countries of the Indian Ocean and the Pacific. Alexander the Great made his way into the Middle East and India in the 300s BCE. The famous Greek historian Herodotus documented not only the conqueror's acts of heroism, but also the corresponding ripple effect of contact and trade with the East, including the infiltration of cotton into the Mediterranean (Crawford 1948: xv).

Linen and wool production both pre-date cotton production, particularly in use for garments. Both materials were more suited to the climates of the Mediterranean, and Central and Northern Europe respectively. Cotton was an import product, and did not really catch on in global trade until the Middle Ages, as medieval shipping routes developed and the textile market expanded. One of the main challenges was finding a way to sell this new material. Often, it was marketed as a substitute for linen, with which European customers were already familiar. In the mean time, India continued to develop the production techniques behind cotton, improving upon weaving and dyeing processes to produce patterns and designs both decorative and utilitarian (Lemire 2013 [1987]: 22).

In 1498, six years after the discovery of the Americas that was credited to Spain's Christopher Columbus, Portuguese explorer Vasco de Gama successfully circumnavigated the African Continent, landing on the coast of India (Lemire [1987] 2013: 21). Portugal then held a dominant role over trade between Asia and Europe for a good portion of the next century (May and Lege 1999: 69). Around 1600, the Dutch and English East India Trading Companies were established, changing the way European markets accessed cotton cloth. As the world grew smaller through the efforts of the famous explorers, the reach of cotton grew larger. As early as 1607, Virginia Colony in the New World was attempting to grow cotton, though North Carolina would find more success with it (May and Lege 1999: 76). Unfortunately, this also began a demand for slave labour – cotton growing and picking was intensive work.

Cotton in the eighteenth and nineteenth centuries

The success of cotton in the early years of the newly formed United States of America can be credited to two factors: the hard work of millions of African slaves, and Eli Whitney's invention of the cotton gin in 1793. Even slave labour was not proving to be a profitable way to complete the labour-intensive process of hand-removing cottonseeds from the raw bolls of cotton fibres. Whitney's gin, with its wire teeth that pulled the cotton against a wire screen to separate the seeds from the lint, increased cotton production exponentially, gradually turning the American South into one of the largest cotton producers in the world (Cohn 1956: 4–16). While America produced a large amount of the raw material, Indian cotton-finished textile goods were still the most sought after cotton product at the turn of the nineteenth century. Chintz, a type of glazed finished cotton, and calico cotton fabrics were incredibly popular in England, leading Parliament to pass several laws throughout the eighteenth century that restricted cotton imports in order to promote the interests of wool farmers. However, demand for these goods was so high that many vendors continued to import the fabrics illegally (Lemire [1987] 2013: 42, 59).

In France, the story was much the same as in England. In the wake of the revolution in the late 1700s, style lines turned to classical inspirations. Fine white cotton muslins were the perfect fabrics to echo the garment designs found on the bleached white marble statues of the idealized classical cultures of Ancient Greece and Rome. With Napoleon looking to revitalize the French economy and French culture, he too partially shut down trade with India, hoping to encourage the rise of the French textile industry. Empress Josephine, however, continued to import heavily embroidered Indian Kashmir wool shawls and finely woven pure white muslins behind her husband's back. These white cotton dresses became the ultimate status symbol for the French elite, as women tried to emulate the empress and showcase their wealth through the purity of the white textile and the many layers of the finest and sheerest cotton muslin available (Tortora and Eubank 2011: 311; Boucher 1987: 339).

The Industrial Revolution finally helped to revitalize the European textile industries in the late eighteenth and early nineteenth centuries. Although Indian cottons were very fine and produced at great quality, the cost of importing made the quantity too low to serve the demand. The first factories were established in England in the mid-1700s, and in 1790 Samuel Slater brought English textile-factory technology to the United States. In spite of laws against exporting the plans or machinery for textile production, Slater established the first US spinning mill from memory in Pawtucket, Rhode Island, in 1790, and expanded the textile-goods production market to the United States (Crawford 1948: xviii; National Cotton Council 1951: 3).

By the 1820s, the US factory system was spreading across the Northeast and changing the economy, as well as the lives of the poor and middle classes. Young women supplied the majority of the labour for the US factory system, using factories and associated dormitory living arrangements such as the ones in Lowell, Massachusetts, as an opportunity to get away from home and earn some money before marriage (Harvard University Library Open Collections Program n.d.). By 1820, there were 102 cotton mills in the United States; by 1831, there were 795; and by 1860, roughly 62,000 women (not to mention men) were employed by the textile factory systems.

The middle of the nineteenth century brought both innovation and chaos to the story of cotton. In 1849, the famous California Gold Rush began, and a small brand known as Levi-Strauss developed. At first, the company created unique work pants made out of heavy canvas for the mining boom, and then switched to indigo-dyed cotton denim. Elements such as riveted pockets and other details associated with the modern Levi's jeans brand evolved later on, as the company prospered and blue jeans rose in popularity among the working classes in many industries. In 1851, Isaac Singer designed the first practical sewing machine, altering the way the garment industry functioned forever. Then in the late 1850s, chemical dyes known as 'aniline' dyes were invented, allowing fabrics to be dyed in more vibrant, bolder colours than ever before (Tortora and Eubank 2011: 356, 358, 361).

After years of tension between the North and the South, the American Civil War erupted in 1861.

This had a profound impact on the economic status of cotton – without the men and slave labour to work the crop and with factories in the North turned to munitions for the war, the global market for American cotton found itself in dire straits. Additionally, in an attempt to manipulate Britain into siding with the Confederate government, 'King Cotton' diplomacy was invented. It was suggested that by destroying or withholding cotton supplies, Britain would have no other choice. Scarcity in supply drove the price of US-grown cotton sky high, somewhere around one dollar per pound, compared to the antebellum average that hovered around 10–15¢ per pound (Cox 1953: 244). While the quality of US cotton was considered to be superior to other sources around the globe, the pull was not so strong that Britain felt the need to support the Confederacy during the war (Dattel 2008; Owsley, Sr 1931; Rodriquez 2000).

New industry officially arrived in the South when the Union won the Civil War. Reconstruction officially ended in 1877, and by 1881, cotton was once again one of the most prominent American industries. The National Cotton Planter's Association organized the International Cotton Exhibition with the blessing of the United States Commissioner of Agriculture, George B. Loring. Hosted in Atlanta, Georgia at Oglethorpe Park, the exhibition covered Southern industries such as sugar, tobacco and rice, though the main focus was on textile manufacturing and cotton production (Loring 1881). The evolution of cotton technology and garment production was on the move yet again.

Though the mid nineteenth century in Europe saw the rise of the couturier Charles Frederick Worth, who focused on highly elaborate, individualized luxury garments; it also created the department store and the beginnings of 'ready-to-wear'. Prior to the 1850s and even after, garments were often created at home from cloth yardage by the women of the household, or made to measure by a tailor or seamstress if the family had the means to pay for the service. As factory systems improved at the end of the century and new technologies for the production of garments evolved, so did the demand for factory-produced cotton garments (Tortora and Eubank 2011: 354, 382; Boucher 1987: 385–86). Catalogues such as Sears, Roebuck and Company or National Cloak and Suit Company offered pages and pages of illustrations, depicting the latest fashions in cotton corset covers, bloomers, petticoats, shirtwaists and nightgowns, as well as eventually the latest ready-to-wear fashions (National Cloak and Suit Company 1992 [1909]).

Cotton in the twentieth century and changing fashions

The turn of the century brought a shift in values and corresponding dressing style that brought pure white cotton back into fashionable prominence. Women were still wearing corsets, but their gowns had slimmed down and become less complicated. Instead of a large two-piece dress requiring multiple layers of petticoats, a bustle and perhaps a cage crinoline to create the proper shape, many dresses were now one piece that hung easily from the shoulders, with a chemise, a light petticoat and a corset underneath for propriety's sake. Though of course materials varied, white cotton was often used for this new style of day dress from roughly 1905 to 1915. The style was commonly called the 'whitework' or 'lingerie' dress, because it looked similar to undergarments (Tortora and Eubank 2011: 425; Boucher 1987: 400).

Sadly, working conditions had only declined since the factory systems were first established in the early 1800s. Many factories were sweatshops where the workers, many of them children or teens, were overworked, underpaid, and not provided proper health care and benefits when injured on the job. In 1911, the tragic Triangle Shirtwaist fire killed 149 women immigrants who had been locked onto the ninth floor to complete their work. Though unions had already started to form,

it would be years before real changes were made to the labour system (Farrell-Beck and Parsons 2007: 34).

World War I disrupted the cotton supply yet again, as noted in the *Journal of Home Economics* in March of 1918. Author Amy L. Rolfe describes how despite growing more than half the cotton in the world, the United States was still struggling with the great demand for uniforms, tent canvas, and cotton gauze and bandages (Tortora and Eubank 2011: 420). As the nation recovered from war in the 1920s, little did they know that cotton would again be in jeopardy with the Stock Market crash and the Great Depression. Not only did the economics of cotton falter, but also over-farming without consideration for soil conservation led to the development of the Dust Bowl across the Southern and Plains states. President Roosevelt's New Deal included a Soil Conservation Service and an Agricultural Adjustment Administration to help cotton farmers rebuild the land and survive the fiscal losses (Hurt 2004).

World War II would be the next challenge to the supply-and-demand forces for the cotton industry. In order to properly supply the troops overseas, General Limitation Order L-85 restricted the amount of silk, rayon, linen and, of course, cotton — material that could be used to create garments. The fashion industry had to creatively design fashionable clothing with small amounts of rationed fabric and subsequently turned towards synthetic fibres. Meanwhile, cotton continued to be churned out and turned into military uniforms with natural strength, durability, washability and absorbency. For the same reasons, indigo-dyed cotton denim overalls or blue jeans were rapidly adopted for war workers on the home front (Farrell-Beck and Parsons 2007: 110–16; National Cotton

Council 1951: 23).

Since their origins, cotton denim blue jeans were seen as a working-class garment, and even in the 1930s and 1940s they were still classified as casual or work wear, suitable for outdoor activities or manual labour. Post-World War II, that image began to change. Fed up with the fallout of the war, a separate youth culture began to evolve under the influence of the zeitgeist and movie characters, like James Dean's from *Rebel Without a Cause*: a sensitive young man craving authenticity in a pair of cuffed denim jeans (Stern et al. 2005). This would begin the dominance of blue jeans in western youth fashions, particularly in the United States, and thus the demand for cotton as denim swept up the social strata from the working classes to Hollywood stars (Sauro 2005: 272–76).

The scientific exploration and innovations begun during World War II did not end with the war. New developments in plastics and extrusion techniques led to the development of more synthetic fibres such as polyester and acrylic, which were invented by Du-Pont in the late 1940s and early 1950s. Cotton would remain a popular choice for some typical products like underwear and towels in the 1950s and 1960s, but in fashion it took a hit from the comparatively easy care and novelty of synthetics. Cotton was also mixed with these new fibres to create blended materials, which ideally took on the best of both fibres' characteristics (Farrell-Beck and Parsons 2007: 147–48).

In order to combat the losses in the cotton market from the success of synthetic fibres, cotton growers successfully petitioned Congress to pass the Cotton Research and Promotion Act of 1966. This act included funding that would establish Cotton Incorporated in 1970, an organization that would lobby fibre mills and the general global public to reap the benefits that cotton had to offer. Though organizations such as the National Cotton Council were already in place, Cotton Incorporated is perhaps the most publicly recognized association outside of the internal industry. Cotton Incorporated successfully branded cotton garments with the 'Seal of Cotton' and advertising campaigns such as the 1989 'The Fabric of Our Lives', which uses the well-known tagline, 'The touch, the feel of cotton, the fabric of our lives' to add a sense of authenticity to the purchase of cotton goods (Cotton Incorporated 2014a).

This campaign was so successful that it was re-launched in 2010 using celebrity endorsers singing the tagline jingle (Cotton Incorporated 2014a). Today, cotton is being evaluated as a natural fibre, one that may be superior to synthetics because of its natural breathability, easy comfort and back-to-nature appeal to millennial customers (Friedman 2015). While synthetics are still very popular, more often than not garments are a mix of fibres, which may include a cotton blend. Moving forward, cotton growers and Cotton Incorporated will have to focus on sustainability as the global community becomes more environmentally conscious, innovating ways to produce this ubiquitous fibre without destroying an even more precious resource: the earth (Cotton Incorporated 2014b).

Conclusion

Cotton has been a part of the human experience for roughly 4,000 years, threading in and out of human history as an import, a luxury commodity, a commonplace fibre, a medical grade material and so much more. Whether working out in the fields, in a factory, in the office or on the runway, cotton is a familiar and often unnoticed presence. Yet this small fibre has a profound influence on the global economy; the corporate system; and the day-to-day life of ordinary people. The true luxury of the cotton fibre is that it can be used in the cheapest T-shirt or the most expensive handbag cover, and it will have an impact. Babies come into this world and are swaddled by cotton, and our loved ones leave this world tucked in just as tight. This fibre certainly has been the fabric of our forefathers, and with innovation it will perhaps be the fabric of our great-grandchildren – but without a doubt, it is indeed 'The Fabric of Our Lives'.

A Visual History of Cotton

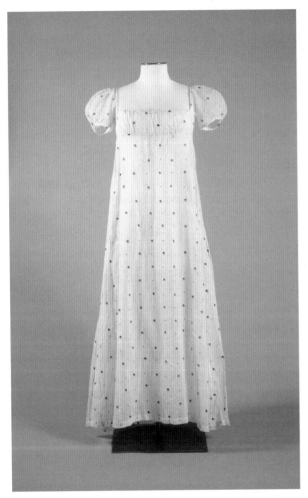

Figure 1: Dress of fine Indian cotton with silver embroidery.
Accession: 62.71.11   Year: *c.*1808
Maker: Unknown   Country: USA
Credit Line: Gift of Mrs William Pleasants

Didactic: This is an evening gown – each of the black spots seen in the photo are actually age-tarnished embroidered silver. At the time, cotton was considered an equally luxurious material as the silver threading through the garment. The finer, sheerer and whiter the cotton, the more fashionable and wealthy the wearer.

Figure 2: Man's roller printed cotton dressing gown.
Accession: 65.79.5   Year: *c.*1820
Maker: Unknown   Country: USA
Credit Line: Gift of Mrs Kenneth S. Gapp

Didactic: The dressing gown was a way for a man to be decent, yet relaxed, while he was at home in the propriety-focused nineteenth and early twentieth centuries. After relinquishing his formal jacket and perhaps his vest, he could even receive male friends in this state of 'undress'.

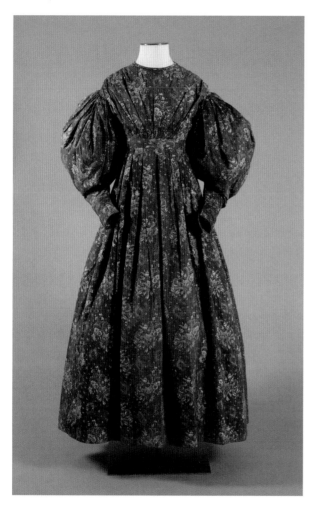

Figure 3: Young woman's dress with gigot sleeves.
Accession: 65.79.1   Year: *c.* 1830
Maker: Unknown   Country: USA
Credit Line: Gift of Mrs Kenneth S. Gapp
Didactic: This simple brown cotton dress with its sloping shoulders, high waistline, and large sleeves is typical for the Romantic period. Within the pattern it is possible to see imperfections to the dye job. This is likely because the fabric was printed using block printing, where instead of hand-painting the fabric, different stamp-like blocks were used to colour in the pattern efficiently, albeit not perfectly.

Figure 4: Woman's roller printed cotton dress.
Accession: 72.23.1   Year: *c.* 1850
Maker: Unknown   Country: USA
Credit Line: Gift of Mrs W. I. Dothard
Didactic: The brilliant colours of this cotton mean it was likely never washed nor worn, miraculously preserving its deep hues. The repeating striped pattern indicates that the textile was printed in a factory. The combination of blue and brown would remain popular until the invention of brighter aniline dyes around 1856–59.

Figure 6: Whitework or Lingerie cotton dress.
Accession: 2014.5.9   Year: *c.*1910
Maker: Unknown   Country: USA
Credit Line: Gift of Annie Williams in memory of Laura Oliver Williams
Didactic: Commonly worn as a light daytime dress, the white cotton lingerie dress was a transition between the heavily corseted styles of the late 1800s and the freer twentieth century. This particular dress is of an even narrower category however – active sportswear. The provenance provided by the donor said that her relative had typically worn the dress to play tennis.

Figure 5: Bustle Period three-piece afternoon dress.
Accession: 87.1.4   Year: *c.*1882
Maker: Unknown   Country: USA
Credit Line: Gift of Mrs Deborah McLaughlin
Didactic: This cotton dress is an excellent early example of **trompe l'œil**. The cotton textile has a pattern that appears to be moiré silk and lace. From far away, it would have seemed to be a much more opulent ensemble, but upon examination the illusion is revealed to be a more inexpensive look.

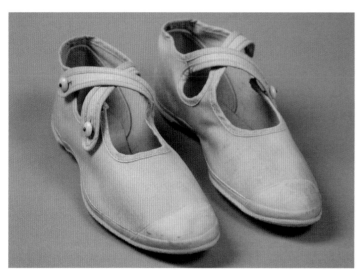

Figure 7: Keds Cotton canvas buttoned sneakers.
Accession: 62.1.1ab   Year: *c.*1925
Maker: Keds   Country: USA
Credit Line: Gift of Mr Harry Cohen and Miss Geraldine Cohen
Didactic: The rubber has long since hardened on this pair of the very
early Keds, perfectly preserving the logo on the soles. Keds began
in 1916 as one of the first brands to produce sneakers. They quickly
became popular with men and women as both genders increasingly
participated in active sports in the 1920s, and collegiate sport culture
infiltrated fashion.

Figure 8: Canvas 'sneaker' wedges patterned with red dots.
Accession: 62.1.2ab   Year: *c.*1940
Maker: Pacemaker Casuals by Wearwell   Country: USA
Credit Line: Gift of Mr Harry Cohen and Miss Geraldine Cohen
Didactic: These darling polka-dot shoes came from the old stock
of Cohen's Family Shoes, a store owned by the donor, the father of
a Drexel Alumnae. The cotton canvas fabric unites the fashionable
wedge shoe with a more utilitarian feel and longevity.

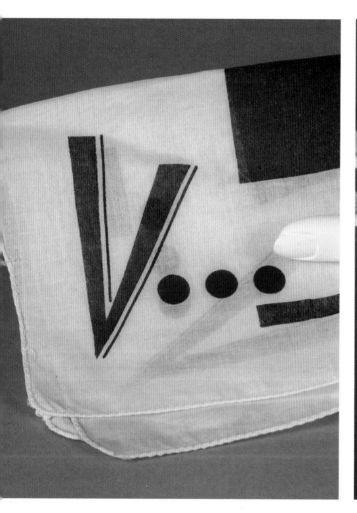

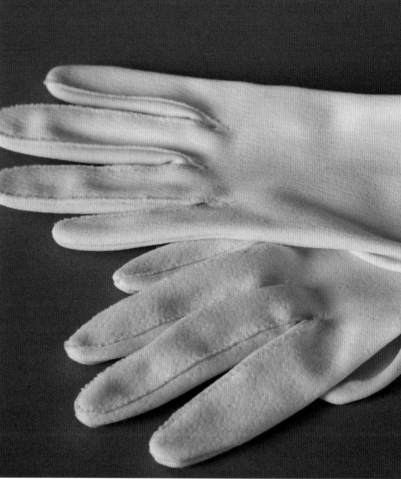

Figure 9: Morse Code handkerchief 'V for Victory'.
Accession: 62.3.88   Year: 1941–45
Maker: Unknown   Country: USA
Credit Line: Gift of Mrs Walter S. Wheeler
Didactic: This cotton handkerchief is only one example of material culture that took the 'V for Victory' Morse code slogan/symbol and fashionably showed support for the troops overseas in World War II. Debuted by the BBC in January of 1941, the letter V was chosen because it was the first letter of the words Victory in French and Freedom in Dutch.

Figure 10: White cotton/nylon gloves with brass buckle.
Accession: 2014.41.9ab   Year: c. 1950
Maker: Unknown   Country: USA
Credit Line: Gift of Suzanne and Keith Orris in honour of Cara Keegan Fry
Didactic: Though plain white cotton gloves were very popular in the 1950s, small details like these brass buckles gave character to a basic staple piece. From the texture of the material, it appears that the cotton has been mixed with nylon, as fibre mixing was an innovation prominent in the post-war years.

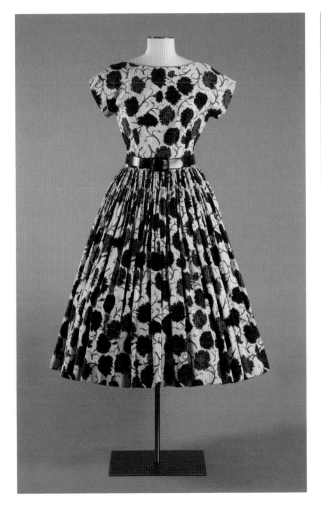

Figure 11: Traina-Norell cotton New Look dress.
Accession: 75.4.4ab   Year: 1954
Maker: Norman Norell   Country: USA
Credit Line: Gift of Mrs Sidney Luce
Didactic: Christian Dior would coin the immortal phrase 'The New Look' for his monumental 1947 collection that showed pinched waists and skirts too full to meet war-time fabric rationing. Here this look is interpreted by American designer Norman Norell in a vivid floral print. Actress Lauren Bacall donated this same garment to the Metropolitan Museum of Art in 1963.

Figure 12: Lilly Pulitzer yellow floral shift dress.
Accession: 2014.13.1   Year: *c.*1963
Maker: Lilly Pulitzer   Country: USA
Credit Line: Gift of Mr and Mrs James B. Bradbeer, Jr
Didactic: The 1960s would come to be defined by a reactionary silhouette – the column. Lilly Pulitzer found a niche in 1960s fashions with her simple but cheerful designs made in brightly coloured prints. Her styles felt fresher and youthful compared to the heavy facade of glamour that 1950s designs often relied upon.

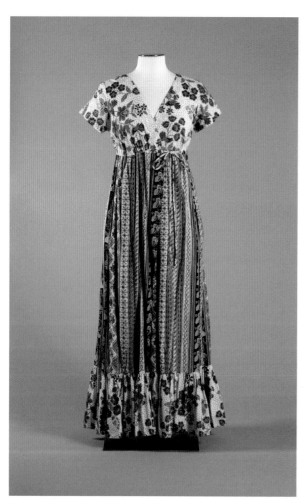

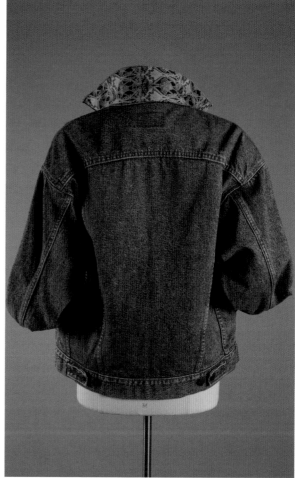

Figure 13: SaraMae patterned cotton jersey wrap nightgown.
Accession: 2009.15.15   Year: *c.*1975
Maker: SaraMae by Lingerie   Country: USA
Credit Line: Gift of Dena Jacobson Dannenberg
Didactic: Cotton has long been a staple in undergarments and lingerie as a fibre known for its breathability and durability. In this nightgown we see a cheerful and friendly mix of patterns combined with a 1970s silhouette for a bohemian, casual take on bedroom wear – both practical and chic for the time.

Figure 14: Levi's denim jacket lined with cotton floral print from Liberty.
Accession: 2015.21.52   Year: *c.*1990
Maker: Levi's and Liberty of London   Country: USA/UK
Credit Line: Gift of Nancy S. Weinberg
Didactic: The combination of these two powerhouse labels that come from such opposite ends of the fashion spectrum is delightfully unexpected. While it looks like just an ordinary denim Levi's jacket, the collar pops up to reveal an intricate art nouveau-inspired Liberty of London print cotton fabric.

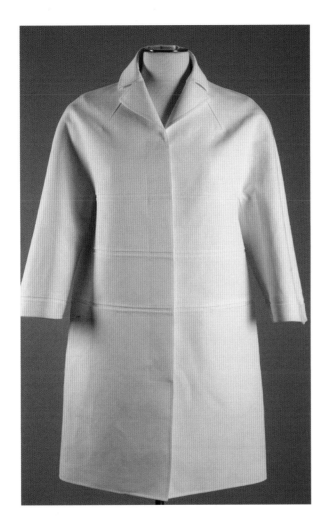

Figure 15: Ralph Rucci tailored coat of 100 per cent cotton with neoprene coating.
Accession: 2014.59.2   Year: **c.** 2000
Maker: Ralph Rucci   Country: USA
Credit Line: Gift of Mrs William McCormick Blair, Jr
Didactic: Ralph Rucci is a designer well noted for his extreme attention to detail and craft. This 100 per cent cotton coat, while simple at first glance, has a stunningly subtle level of construction that feels completely futuristic, once again taking cotton from ordinary to extraordinary.

Acknowledgements

I owe a huge debt of gratitude to the Robert and Penny Fox Historic Costume Collection at Drexel University (FHCC) for the use of their objects and photo studio. Thank you particularly to Archives Specialist Michael Shepherd and Collections Manager Monica Stevens Smyth for their assistance with this project.

All mannequin dressing was completed by the author with the assistance of FHCC Curator Clare Sauro, without whom this would not have been possible. All photographs provided courtesy of Virginia Theerman.

Thanks are also due to the American Textile History Museum staff in Lowell, Massachusetts, specifically Curator Karen Herbaugh and Librarian Jane Ward, for their assistance with research for this project and for their kindness to a fledgling researcher.

Of course, my thanks go to Dr Joseph H. Hancock, II, for his continual faith in my abilities as a writer and researcher. Thank you for this opportunity.

References

Boucher, François (1987), *20,000 Years of Fashion: The History of Costume and Personal Adornment*, New York: Harry N. Abrams, Inc. Publishers.

Brown, D. Clayton (2011), *King Cotton in Modern America: A Cultural, Political, and Economic History since 1945*, Jackson: University of Mississippi Press.

Burkett, Charles William and Poe, Clarence Hamilton (1906), *Cotton: Its Cultivation, Marketing, Manufacture, and the Problems of the Cotton World*, New York: Doubleday, Page & Company.

Cox, Alonzo Bettis (1953), *Cotton: Demand, Supply, Merchandising*, Austin: Hemphill's.

Cohn, David L. (1956), *The Life and Times of King Cotton*, New York: Oxford University Press.

Cotton Incorporated (2014a), 'Cotton Incorporated's History: 1960–1969', http://www.cottoninc.com/corporate/About-Cotton-Incorporated/Cotton-Incorporated-company-history/timeline.1960-1969.cfm. Accessed 15 June 2015.

Cotton Incorporated (2014b), 'Cotton Today', http://www.cottoninc.com/sustainability/CottonToday/index.cfm. Accessed 15 June 2015.

Crawford, M. D. C. (1948), *The Heritage of Cotton: The Fibre of Two Worlds and Many Ages*, New York: Fairchild Publishing Company.

Dattel, Eugene R. (2008), 'Cotton and the Civil War', *Mississippi History Now*, http://mshistorynow.mdah.state.ms.us/articles/291/cotton-and-the-civil-war. Accessed 15 June 2015.

DeBlois, Diane and Harris, Robert Dalton (2008), 'Morse Code V for Victory: Morale through the Mail in WWII', *Smithsonian National Postal Museum*, http://postalmuseum.si.edu/Symposium2008/DeBlois-Harris-V_for_Victory-paper.pdf. Accessed 15 June 2015.

Farrell-Beck, Jane and Parsons, Jean (2007), *Twentieth Century Dress in the United States*, New York: Fairchild Publications, Inc.

Friedman, Arthur (2015), 'Cotton Incorporated Gets Authentic for Latest Ads', *WWD: Women's Wear Daily*, http://wwd.com/media-news/fashion-memopad/cotton-incorporated-ads-10112969/. Accessed 15 June 2015.

Harvard University Library Open Collections Program (n.d.), 'Lowell and Lawrence Textile Mills', *Women Working, 1800–1930*, http://ocp.hul.harvard.edu/ww/mills.html. Accessed 15 June 2015.

Hurt, R. Douglas (2004), 'Dust Bowl', in Robert S. McElvaine (ed.), *Encyclopedia of the Great Depression*, vol. 1, New York: Macmillan Reference USA, http://ic.galegroup.com/ic/uhic/ReferenceDetailsPage/DocumentToolsPortletWindow?displayGroupName=Reference&action=2&catId=-GALE%7C00000000MXIM&documentId=GALE%7C-CX3404500149&source=Bookmark&u=mlin_c_montytech&jsid=900bdba6ad8b529cd4cbb66a6b8365fc. Accessed 15 June 2015.

Lemire, Beverly ([1987] 2013), *Cotton*, London: Bloomsbury Academic.

Loring, George B., et al (1881), *Address of Hon. George B. Loring, Commissioner of Agriculture, and other proceedings of the Cotton Convention held in Atlanta, Ga. November 2, 1881*. https://archive.org/stream/addressofhongeor17lori#page/n3/mode/2up. Accessed 15 June 2015.

May, O. L. and Lege, K. E. (1999), 'Development of the World Cotton Industry', in C. Wayne Smith and J. Tom Cothren (eds), *Cotton: Origin, History, Technology, and Production*, New York: John Wiley & Sons, Inc. pp. 65–97.

Metropolitan Museum of Art Online Collection (n.d.), '"Dress" [C.I.63.10a, b] by Norman Norell, 1954. Gift of Miss Lauren Bacall, 1963]', http://www.metmuseum.org/collection/the-collection-online/search/97271?rpp=30&pg=1&ft=norell&what=Cotton&pos=17. Accessed 15 June 2015.

National Cloak and Suit Company ([1909] 1992), *Women's Fashions of the Early 1900s: An Unabridged Republication of New York Fashions, 1909*, New York: Dover Publications.

National Cotton Council of America (1951), *Cotton from Field to Fabric*, New York: National Cotton Council.

National Cotton Council of America (2015), 'About the National Cotton Council', http://www.cotton.org/about/index.cfm. Accessed 15 June 2015.

Owsley Sr, Frank Lawrence (1931), *King Cotton Diplomacy: Foreign Relations of the Confederate States of America*, Tuscaloosa: University of Alabama Press.

Rodriquez, A. (2000), 'Cotton', in *Encyclopedia of the American Civil War: A Political, Social, and Military History*, Santa Barbara, CA: ABC-CLIO.

Sauro, Clare (2005), 'Jeans', in Valerie Steele (ed.), *Encyclopedia of Clothing and Fashion*, vol. 2, Detroit: Charles Scribner's Sons, pp. 272–76.

Stern, S., et al. (2005), *Rebel Without a Cause*, Burbank, CA: Warner Home Video.

Tortora, Phyllis G. and Eubank, Keith (2011), *Survey of Historic Costume: A History of Western Dress*, 5th ed., New York: Fairchild Books.

Appcessories Democratically Disrupting
Domestic Production through Innovation

Sarah Portway

Introduction

This is the story of Appalatch, an innovative retailer and textile manufacturer perched in the mountains of North Carolina. From its online retail platform, the company offers a diverse range of classic American products, from T-shirts and sweaters to socks and blankets. Co-founders Grace Gouin and Mariano deGuzman aim to make Appalatch an ethically and sustainably driven outdoor apparel company, and they have infused every aspect of their business with a rebellious spirit. They are on a mission to revolutionize and democratize the American clothing industry, one custom-made sweater at a time. The revolution: Appalatch is the first company in the world to harness available knitwear technology to develop (and patent) a mass-customized-sweater-making process. The democratization: it keeps prices low and wages fair by cutting out the middlemen. It collaborates directly with the farmers, mill- and factory workers within its supply chain, and it offers finished products directly to the consumer via its website. No distribution centres, no warehouses, no complex global supply chains. Just honestly made, timeless American clothing of exceptional quality and durability, with a perfectly customized fit every time.

A brief history

Appalatch produces their premium cotton sweaters inside the 'Living-Wage Certified' EchoView Fiber Mill in Weaverville, just outside Asheville, North Carolina. EchoView is also the only 'LEED Gold Certified' fibre-processing mill in world. Seeking these

Figure 1: The Stoll CMS 822 HP multi-gauge knitting machine. (Photo by Sarah Portway.)

certifications for their manufacturing site stemmed logically from the core values that hatched Appalatch in 2012, and these values are evident from the threshold. This collaborative space houses most of the domestic manufacturing facilities that have allowed the growing company to vertically integrate production. The design-studio window overlooks the sky-lit fibre-processing floor and the founders can easily find experts in the building to ask questions, access resources (such as costly humidity controlled yarn-storage space), and connect with a growing list of American fibre suppliers. Cooperation comes naturally to Appalatch. Since the beginning, co-founder and CEO Mariano deGuzman matched his Harvard Business background with co-founder and Creative Director Grace Gouin's design expertise, acquired at Skidmore College. The two are building something unique, and that requires a diverse but complementary set of skills.

During the first year, the duo was focused on building a responsible and honest supply chain by locating key people and suppliers themselves. This necessitated travelling and partnering directly with the mills and farms that grow and process their raw materials, like Arch Woodward's sheep farm in Montana. Arch was a shepherd without a herd, until Ms Gouin and Mr deGuzman met him. Appalatch determined that Rambouillet wool had the optimal properties they sought and purchased the wool upfront so that Arch could reliably build his livestock around their needs (Start Up TV Show 2014). By ordering their fibres and paying up-front, Appalatch is rebelliously establishing a reliable income stream for American farmers, bucking the industry trend of low-cost sourcing. Every link in the supply chain can be traced back to an individual, and every individual is an integral cog in the Appalatch machine. Every hand that touches an Appalatch material is cared for in an empathetic and responsible way because they are directly connected to the founders. As Appalatch has grown and expanded their fibre offerings to include cotton, these values have remained firmly embedded in the culture of the company.

The business model
It took a full year to build their innovative supply chain, but by 2013 Appalatch had already turned a profit. In true democratic spirit, initial funding was a combination of personal-, family- and crowd-sourced investments. With $55,000 raised on Kickstarter, Ms Gouin and Mr deGuzman acquired a Stoll CMS 822 HP multi-gauge knitting machine, which they compare to a 3D printer for textiles. The technology is cutting edge and the process has been patented, but prices are still kept lower than comparable products because virtually no waste is produced. Each component of a customer's custom-fitted sweater is made to measure, there are no leftover sizes to sell at the end of the season, and there is little to no yarn wasted in production. This allows Appalatch to invest in more luxurious yarns because the wasted material can fit in the palm of Ms Gouin's hand. At EchoView, this waste can be recycled into other fibre products such as stuffing or roving.

In a personal interview, Mr deGuzman explained, 'We are trying to connect people to the way clothing is made'. Their proprietary software acts as a conduit between customer and machine. This technology did not exist ten years ago, and Appalatch is leading the way. In a personal interview, Ms Gouin explained that 'technology can take an ancient fibre and turn it into something that is modern, fashionable, and that you want to wear; and it can eliminate that handmade element that is back-breaking'. By eliminating a large part of the work usually done by hand in traditional cut-and-sew manufacturing, Appalatch is able to offer competitive pricing on American-made goods while still paying their production team a living wage.

At full capacity, with the three staff members working a 40-hour work week, Appalatch can create 6,000 custom-sweaters per year, or twenty per week. All employees switch tasks throughout their shifts to keep things interesting, and long lunches or yoga breaks are often part of a typical workday.

The short road from wool to cotton
Appalatch is known for their made-to-measure, do-

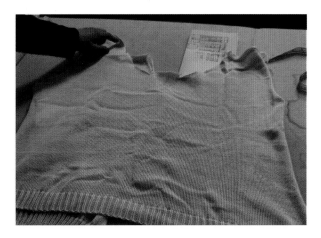

Figure 2: A pre-formed, custom-fitted cotton sweater component is inspected after knitting, before assembly and washing. Washing changes the stitch density of these components; they appear shorter and wider before washing compared to the final product. (Photo by Sarah Portway.)

mestically sourced wool sweaters. Because Appalatch is still producing in a relatively small volume, these wool sweaters can be increasingly 'hyper-local'. Appalatch recently started purchasing yarns from EchoView, whose sheep live happily across the road from its shared facilities. But in a personal interview, Ms Gouin explained, 'we're not purists'. Appalatch is not a one-fibre brand, and it continues to collaborate with yarn innovators on research and development. The founders believe that using diverse materials for their products creates optimal sustainability potential, but most importantly, Mr deGuzman states, 'we want to support farmers here in the United States'.

A preference for hyper-local sourcing has lead Appalatch to use cotton from the Carolinas. Finding cotton grown in America was easy, and the price per yard for cotton (approximately $8 per yard) is considerably lower than wool (approximately $16 per yard). Since yarn cost is a pivotal factor in the custom sweater's final retail price, the team is thrilled that the newly launched cotton sweater will allow for more democratic retail offerings from this premium brand.

Negotiating the organic landscape

Appalatch has previously offered accessories and base layers made from Cotton of the Carolinas (a collaboration of farmers and manufacturers dedicated to growing, making and selling cotton T-shirts in the Carolinas). When the brand expanded their sweater offerings and

required a new organic cotton source, they needed to negotiate value. The cotton available through its usual hyper-local inroads was suitable for T-shirts, but was not the quality or staple length required for the machine-knit sweaters. In a personal interview, Mariano deGuzman said:

For us sustainability is a mixture of different things, and a large part of that has to do with how long this piece of clothing will exist […] we don't want our clothing to break down, we don't want any of this planned obsolescence stuff, so we want to use the highest quality fibre and yarn possible, and hopefully we can find someone that is the most responsible at that. Buhler is that.

Buhler owns processing facilities in both the United States and Switzerland. Although Buhler's Jefferson, Georgia, facilities are local to Appalatch, they are not certified organic. In order to certify the fibre-processing mill, every square inch would need to be thoroughly cleaned and detailed from floor tiles to air ducts. Domestic demand for certified organic cotton has not yet allowed Buhler to make this costly switch, although American companies like Appalatch have a big role to play in making this switch financially viable. Once the demand for local organic cotton makes business sense in America, the facilities will come, says Ms Gouin. So, the Supima cotton used in an Appalatch custom-fit sweater is grown in California, shipped to Switzerland for Buhler's certified organic processing,

Figure 3: The front and back of a custom-fitted cotton sweater is stitched together by hand using a linking machine. (Photo by Sarah Portway.)

Figure 4: The ends of each seam are woven back into the final garment by hand. (Photo by Sarah Portway.)

and then shipped back to North Carolina for manufacturing. When less travelled organic cotton is possible, Appalatch will support it. They are on the forefront of the demand and optimistic that this carbon trade-off is temporary.

The customer experience

A person who purchases a sweater from Appalatch can be a responsible consumer without paying a higher price for comparable quality. Mr deGuzman describes their clothing as a long-term investment, which rebels against the disposable fashion currently being channelled into over-flowing landfills. Appalatch clothes will stand the test of time, both in materials and design aesthetic. They emphasize these qualities of longevity and timelessness on their website by featuring a classic, well-fitted crew-neck knitted sweater from decades in the distant past up to the present day.

Ms Gouin lovingly describes the superior connection and unity the wearer feels when a garment is custom-fit. When a customer is emotionally invested in the garment, they will keep it forever. Customers submit four key measurements when making their purchase to get the right fit: sleeve length, torso length,

chest circumference and waist circumference. They can take this measurement on their body, or from a favourite garment they already own. Their sweater will arrive at their door one week after they order.

How it's made

Making a customized cotton sweater only takes two hours at Appalatch, thanks to their patented process. Measurements are fed through the Stoll 822 knitting machine (see Figure 1), which creates pre-formed sweater components without the need for any additional cutting (see Figure 2). This simultaneously reduces labour and material costs. The pre-formed sweater components are then hand-fed through a linking machine (see Figure 3). Linking is difficult and relatively slow handwork compared to the alternatives, but Ms Gouin prefers the linked-seam quality and longevity. Finally, the ends of the seams are hand-finished (see Figure 4). Because the yarns need to be waxed before passing through the knitting machine, all sweaters are washed and dried for softness before being shipped to the customer.

Figure 5: The Appalatch team (from left to right): Mariano deGuzman, Jr, Grace Gouin, Allyson Ansusinha, Dezi deGuzman and Ramel deGuzman. (Photo by Sarah Portway.)

The future

The future of Appalatch looks bright. They hope to grow their business from one to eighty knitting machines over the next five years. They are already talking over the difficult choices they will face so they can grow towards their goals, rather than being forced to make difficult in-the-moment decisions, which often lead to a slippage in business standards. The small team is growing (see Figure 5), and they are building an honest business from the ground up, right in our backyard.

References

Appalatch (2012), 'Our Story', http://appalatch.com/pages/this-is-where-our-story-begins. Accessed 21 February 2015.

Start Up TV Show (2014), 'Appalatch | Start Up TV Show, Season 2, Episode 7.1', https://www.youtube.com/watch?v=du-vsZwnk-dA&feature=youtube_gdata_player. Accessed 14 December 2015.

Made in the USA: Spotlight on Fashions Unlimited

Shahidah Hasan

Introduction

Fashion apparel production in the United States has experienced tumultuous times; however, companies such as Fashions Unlimited remain at the forefront of product development and innovation. Although China has had a tremendous impact on manufacturing in the United States, a number of fashion companies and major brands such as Diane von Furstenberg, Coach, Nanette Lepore and Nicole Miller produce a percentage of their collections in the United States. For most of these brands, Fashions Unlimited is the company managing the production and development of their products that are 'Made in the USA'. Fashions Unlimited owner Philip Spector has worked with brands and special projects and partnered with students to support the next generation of production connoisseurs.

Fashions Unlimited is equipped for producing, auditing and developing conglomerate products for reputable fashion companies. His company may be considered a small- to medium-sized enterprise, but his skill set in design and pattern development, as well as his experience in third-party product audits for companies such as Under Armour, have allowed him to remain competitive in a volatile market. Mr Spector mentioned that he did business with one particular customer on a handshake for twelve years. Being in this industry for many years, Mr Spector has seen dramatic changes in the culture that have caused the company to change the way it conducts business. Mr Spector believes that people lack knowledge of the industry and that there is very little loyalty and integrity. Trust has become a major challenge in his business and he currently requires his customers to pay for their merchandise before it is distributed. Years ago, you could trust a company to send payment based on discussions and the handshake. Subsequently to Asian business principles, you create lifelong partnerships through trust, integrity and commitment to completing the work.

Philip Spector was an English major in college. Upon graduating, he went to California and lived there for eighteen months before returning to Philadelphia, Pennsylvania, to begin his career in fashion. He landed a position loading and unloading fabric until he began working at Gimbels. Lit Brothers and Gimbels were three established retailers at 8th and Market Streets in Philadelphia, a prominent hub for fashion and retail. Today, Century 21 occupies the space that was once a retail landmark.

Gimbels's history began in rural Vincennes, Indiana, where Bavarian immigrant Adam Gimbel opened his first dry goods establishment in the 1840s. As Gimbels became successful in Milwaukee, Adam Gimbel's sons began to identify new markets. They decided that Philadelphia would give their store immediate access to the East Coast market. In 1983, the Gimbel brothers bought Haines and Company, a dry goods store, for $1 million. The store reopened as Gimbels Philadelphia on 21 March 1984. Mr Spector made his start with Gimbels by loading and unloading fabrics. He then started working with London Fog, a well-

Figure 1: Fashions Unlimited production space. (Photo by Nioka N. Wyatt.)

known global lifestyle brand founded by Israel Myers in 1923. The first London Fog store opened in the 1970s, and the company produced two-thirds of all raincoats sold in the United States. Mr Spector worked with the company for nine years and streamlined his career into manufacturing. Based on his past experiences, Mr Spector believes that employees should be cross-trained in order to manage a variety of daily duties. This maximizes knowledge-sharing and problem-solving when employees face any challenges that arise.

After working for various manufacturers, Philip Spector decided to take his knowledge of the industry and develop his own company. In August 1976, Mr Spector created Fashions Unlimited. Since its founding, the company has built a reputation in the industry for its attention to detail and ability to produce quality products. Mr Spector can vividly remember when business was conducted on a handshake. Today, business is conducted through a series of negotiations, paperwork and dishonesty – which makes it difficult for small businesses to remain competitive.

Throughout the years, he has partnered with companies such as Adidas, not only on product development ventures, but also to produce a wide array of cotton merchandise. He attributes the growth and development of cotton to Cotton Incorporated's constant marketing, an area he is seeking to develop in his business model. Fashions Unlimited is represented on a minute list of full-service apparel contractors that offer products 'Made in the USA'. This concept is indicative of developing quality products, but also supports production companies that have invested financially and socially in localization.

Operational challenges

How can a small company such as Fashions Unlimited remain competitive?

Although Fashions Unlimited is known for its impeccable work and diversity, the company has experienced tumultuous times. China's manufacturing

Figure 2: Production facility in Hellam, Pennsylvania. (Photo Courtesy of Fashions Unlimited.)

principles created a means of disruptive challenges, but the comeback of US manufacturing has also faced industry opposition. It is difficult to find skilled labour, and those who are new to the industry are seeking promotion after only a few months of employment. Nonetheless, they are not willing to begin their career loading and unloading trucks. Subsequently, the majority of his employees have worked with him for ten or more years. Mr Spector believes that his company has survived because of its honesty and ability to engage in product development and diverse projects. The product portfolio at Fashions Unlimited consists of woven and knitted dresses; skirts, tops and pants; and it specializes in swimwear. One of Mr Spector's primary materials used in developing his private line of girl's dresses was cotton.

The fabric offers increased comfort and durability and is easier to manage in the production cycle. In addition, Jessica Simpson, Coach and Diane von Furstenberg recognize his noteworthy skill in swimwear production and have worked with Fashions Unlimited on developing new lines and product assortments. Most of the communication with clients is conducted via e-mail, but old-school phone communication goes a long way. Prior to partnering with clients, Mr Spector requires them to attend an initial visit to cultivate the business relationship. When Mr Spector meets with clients, he listens to them and if they are not truly willing to devote time and effort to their product, he will not work with them. In fact, this company turns down a lot of work due to clients' lack of knowledge or commitment to their projects. While most companies charge a flat rate, Fashions Unlimited charges by the hour. Mr Spector believes that this is a more honest way of charging the customer. The majority of Fashions Unlimited customers are referred by word of mouth. Mr Spector does not have a significant budget for advertising. He believes that his work and knowledge speak more than what he can place on a billboard. However, this year Mr Spector began to send flyers to potential customers via e-mail to market his current focus for his company: product development.

Company structure

Fashions Unlimited has two locations: Baltimore, Maryland and Hellam, Pennsylvania. Mr Spector decided to open the company in Maryland because that is where he found work after completing school. The Pennsylvania location opened based on a business opportunity that was presented to him when the Danskin Company closed. Fashions Unlimited moved into its current office space in Baltimore in 1994. Previously, its space was across the hall in the same building and was considerably larger than the space it currently occupies. The Baltimore location handles development such as pattern-making, sourcing and line development. The Pennsylvania location is equipped to handle large-scale production and special projects. There are challenges with maintaining two different locations, but he prefers to have multiple locations that specialize in product development and mass production. For example, the company completed work for Homeland Security for twelve years in the same facility. Although Mr Spector spends time at both locations, he credits his staff for streamlining communication and special projects. Both locations have a full line of employees with staff and managers. The manager who oversees production has worked with Mr Spector for over 36 years. There are two other key employees who work at Fashions Unlimited. One is a graduate of Virginia Tech and the other is a graduate of Philadelphia University and manages product development and design strategy. Mr Spector believes that all his employees must be versatile. The more information they know about all areas of the industry, the better they will perform. Since it is a small-scale operation, if an employee is working on another project, someone else can fulfil other duties and obligations through cross-training and pollination.

In addition to the Baltimore and the Hellam locations, Mr Spector operates a knitting facility in Charlotte, North Carolina, called American Seamless Knitting. This location is a circular knitwear facility, with a full-service development lab that features Santoni 28 gauge jacquard circular knitting machines in 13", 15" and 17" machine cylinder sizes. This division has done work for well-known athletic apparel companies such as Adidas, Lululemon and Reebok, and is primarily a resource centre for product development and innovation.

Services

One attribute that is very important to Fashions Unlimited is the ability to perform whatever jobs the customer desires. The company offers a wide range of services such as product development, pattern making, cutting, sewing, reworking, pressing, finishing and consultations. It has an extensive list of clients which includes some of the world's most reputable brands, such as Adidas, Coach, Diane von Furstenberg, J. Crew, Nike, Oscar de la Renta and Under Armour. In fact, during a speaking engagement at Philadelphia University, Mr Spector's Adidas clients spoke highly of his ability to create patterns and identify potential problems before production. The team noted that there are very few companies knowledgeable in producing knits and woven products; most of the facilities are specialized and their employees are not trained properly. Though Fashions Unlimited is not equipped to produce denim, it has an array of machinery that allows for a range of products. For example, it has the ability to implement seam sealing, which allows a garment to become waterproof. This particular machine aligns the tape with the seams to protect the wearer during extreme weather conditions. In the production process, if the machine becomes too hot the fabric will melt. This machine was used to work on the extreme weather garments used for the Mount Everest climb, a special project that Mr Spector worked on in 2010.

Quality control

Quality control is another service that Fashions Unlimited has added to its portfolio. In the past, the company has worked with National Geographic to evaluate the quality of garments made overseas. Despite the fact that technical packets were distributed, quality issues were found while evaluating the products. Technical packets include the necessary elements for producing products such as construction details, measurement specs, care instructions, fibre content and a sketch of the product.

Figure 3: Jacket developed for extreme weather conditions. (Photo Courtesy of Fashions Unlimited.)

Fashions Unlimited has also been known to rework inferior products made by other countries. Another special project that Fashions Unlimited embarked on was with a children's-wear company that produced garments made with rhinestones overseas. The products contained a high volume of lead contamination and so were not shipped to customers. Fortunately, Mr Spector's team was able to remove all of the rhinestones and reapplied the products with uncontaminated rhinestones.

Mr Spector partnered with Textronics, a start-up company that was acquired by Adidas. At the time, there was a lack of standards for wiring on wearable technology. These garments were challenging, and other manufacturers were not comfortable with committing to this type of job. They did not want the liability that comes along with conductive textile material applications. But where other manufacturers were apprehensive, Fashions Unlimited welcomed the opportunity and embraced the challenge. Mr Spector's team assisted with wiring the prototypes and testing the products. The Textronics team is located close to Mr Spector's facility in Pennsylvania. This allowed his team to remain hands-on, conduct testing and complete fittings on a consistent basis. Mr Spector did everything in-house and followed the projects all the way through with accuracy. Fashions Unlimited continued to work with Textronics after it became a part of the Adidas team.

Production capabilities

At Fashions Unlimited, there are no minimums required to take on a project. There is a three-week turnaround time for 430 pieces. It has been working with a small company based in Seattle that produces Mastectomy Bras since 2000. Fashions Unlimited takes pride in being highly diverse and in taking on the smallest to the most complicated jobs. Over the years, it has worked with many large-scale apparel companies doing high-volume work. Mr Spector and his team

worked with Danskin for many years. Danskin started out in the 1800s as the go-to company for tights and leotards for dancers in New York City. Over the years, the company evolved to produce fashionable, functional dancewear, activewear and casual clothes, as well as fitness equipment. Fashions Unlimited also worked with what was one of the largest women's brands during the 1970s to the mid-1990s: Liz Claiborne. Liz Claiborne provided the patterns and Fashions Unlimited completed the garments with essential cotton materials and trim applications.

Competitors

One of the main challenges for US-based production facilities is remaining competitive and offering reasonable prices. American businesses, including Fashions Unlimited, have endured the disruptive trend of distributing work overseas. However, when it comes to working with materials such as stretch fabrics, Mr Spector and his staff consider companies in California their largest competitors. Some of the companies are operating without the proper regulations. These types of operations pay wages 'under the table' and, regardless of the amount of work, the employees are guaranteed a set pay every week. These unregulated businesses operate as sweatshops and create challenges for production companies.

Philanthropy

During one semester, Mr Spector collaborated with Philadelphia University as a way to give back to the younger generation looking for a career path in the fashion industry. Fashions Unlimited produced all the garments for the students in the Global Fashion Insight class. The term project provided hands-on experience for students to develop a fashion company and create a line of fashion products. The purpose of the project was for students to create companies within the class, produce fifteen or more units of a fashion product, and sell the products at a pop-up shop on campus. The students were required to study the business of fashion while engaging in elements of supply-chain management. In addition, they learned costing methods and how to collaborate with a team. Each company consisted of a CEO while others collaborated in Design and Merchandising, Marketing and Interactive Technology, and Production. The products were showcased at a pop-up store located on the campus and proceeds were donated to Chemo Clothes, an organization that supports victims experiencing financial hardship due to cancer.

Future outlook of Fashions Unlimited

Fashions Unlimited has maintained its business by producing quality merchandise for leading fashion companies. The company is not only knowledgeable of vast areas in the supply-chain system, but equipped with the skills necessary to support fashion companies in product development, auditing, and developing best practices for producing cotton products. One of the consistent attributes of Phil and his team at Fashions Unlimited are their ability to work on diverse projects, materials and products. Few manufacturers are equipped to develop such a range of products – from delicate cotton undergarments to technical garments, like extreme weather gear – with such accuracy and precision. Although Mr Spector has suffered his fair share of challenges, he has a positive outlook on production in the United States and on the next generation of fashion leaders. His compelling record of supporting the fashion industry on major projects at area universities is a small testament to his compassion and long-standing leadership abilities. Perhaps more telling is the positive organizational culture that he employs at Fashions Unlimited.

Introduction

Tara St James is the founder of Study NY, an ethical contemporary women's wear brand that is based in Brooklyn, New York. Tara St. James's business model embodies slow fashion ideals such as small-scale and local production of high quality clothing made for extended use. Study NY is a leader in slow fashion, as it applies zero-waste design strategies for the creation of timeless and versatile clothing. Clothing patterns are carefully crafted to use the entire length and width of the fabric and eliminate textile waste in the supply chain.

Study NY's approach to clothing production is a shift away from the traditional wholesale apparel business-model that relies on fashion trends, mass production and optimal consumption patterns. Tara St James developed the 'Anti-Fashion Calendar' in 2013 as an alternative to traditional clothing production processes, which her business initially began with in 2010. The 'Anti-Fashion Calendar' promotes small-scale production throughout the year to consistently support the local clothing and textiles economy.

The 'Uniform Collection' of Study NY revolves around four staple designs. Each clothing style is produced in batches of 50 to 100. Tara recreates successful styles with slight alterations. Study NY uses organic cotton in approximately 80 per cent of the 'Uniform Collection'. Organic cotton is sourced from the United States, Turkey, India and Egypt; fibres are processed into fabric in the United States, China, Japan and India. A key motivation for using organic cotton is reducing the chemical impact of the Study NY supply chain.

Organic cotton farm-to-fashion supply chain

Organic cotton uses no synthetic or chemical pesticides, insecticides, fertilizers or genetically modified organisms (Textile Exchange 2014). In 2014, the United States was the fifth leading producer of organic cotton, after India, China, Turkey and Tanzania (Textile Exchange 2015).[1] Leading organic cotton producers in the United States are Texas, Arizona, California, New Mexico and North Carolina (OTA 2015).[2] The amount of land devoted to organic cotton in the United States has steadily increased since 2003. In 2014, the acreage allocated for organic cotton was the largest since 1995 – a 14 per cent increase of 18,234 acres. In 2013, organic cotton yields were 10,335 bales, a 17 per cent increase compared to 2012. Although drought has been a prevailing threat to cotton cultivation in recent years, in 2013 the main environmental factors affecting the crop were severe wind and hail. The Organic Trade Association (OTA) predicts continued growth of the organic cotton industry in the United States.

Texas Organic Cotton Marketing Cooperative in Lubbock, Texas

A majority of domestic cotton is cultivated in the

Figure 1: Zero-waste kimono tunic dress, made of hemp and organic cotton, from Study NY's Uniform collection. (Photo by Sacha Maric.)

Southern Plains of Texas in Lubbock, which is known as the 'world's largest cotton patch'. The weather conditions and terrain make the region ideal for cultivating cotton. LaRhea Pepper, current managing director of Textile Exchange, was one of the founders of the Texas Organic Cotton Marketing Cooperative (TOCMC) in 1993. Ms Pepper initiated relationships with large fashion brands to create a market for domestic organic cotton.

TOCMC was developed to assist farmers reach a market with organic cotton. Kelly Pepper, manager of TOCMC, explains, 'The volume of organic cotton is very small even as a cooperative. It's better to market the cotton all together rather than market as individuals'. The cooperative combines the cotton from 35 organic cotton family farms in the region and aids with marketing on a larger scale.

Organic cotton farms are certified by the USDA National Organic Program. Each cotton bale is tracked from field to customer with the name of the farm. The greatest yield of organic cotton for the TOCMC was in 2007 with 15,000 bales. In 2014, approximately 19,000 acres were devoted to organic cotton with a harvest of 10,000 bales. Kelly Pepper indicated that 1,000 bales were in 'transition' to become fully 'organic'. To be considered organic, the farm has to eliminate chemical use on the cotton for a three-year period. 'Transition' is the time-period of change from being a 'conventional' to an 'organic' cotton producer.

Texas organic cotton farmers face several challenges. The drought over the past four years has reduced overall production. The abundant weeds, severe wind and snow also affect the quality and quantity of organic cotton. Farmers also risk pesticide contamination from other farms.

Kelly Pepper indicates that domestic organic cotton is a 'niche within a niche'. Less than 1 per cent of worldwide cotton is organic and the United States grows a small portion of it. The United States has a higher premium of organic cotton compared to other countries that have lower prices. The market for organic cotton is small and is predominantly apparel companies committed to producing products domestically. Since there is a limited supply of organic cotton, companies that have existing relationships with TOCMC are prioritized. A key company in the farm-to-fabric supply chain is Spiritex, who facilitates the production of the fibre to fabric for clothing production in the United States.

Spiritex in Asheville, North Carolina

Spiritex bridges the gap between the fibre community and fashion industry. Daniel Sanders co-founded Spiritex in 2005. When the TOCMC organic cotton is ready for processing, Spiritex coordinates a domestic supply chain for fabric production within a 150-mile radius of Asheville, North Carolina. Spinning is completed in the Hill Spinning Mill in Thomasville, North Carolina; knitting on circular machines in Clover, South Carolina; and finishes such as scouring, bleaching or dyeing are completed in Lincolnton, North Carolina.

According to Daniel, 150,000 pounds of fabrics are produced annually and organic cotton makes up 80 to 85 per cent of the fabric output.[3] Study NY sources a small amount of organic cotton fabric when compared to the total fabric produced by Spiritex. As the bridge between organic cotton farms, fabric producers and designers, Spiritex is a fundamental supplier that makes domestic farm-to-fashion with organic cotton possible.

Brooklyn Fashion Designer Accelerator in Brooklyn, New York

The Study NY farm-to-fashion supply chain converges in New York City with organic cotton sourced from Texas and fabric manufactured in the Carolinas. Initial clothing samples are created by Tara St James in the Brooklyn Fashion Designer Accelerator (BFDA) studio and produced in the Fashion District of New York City.

BFDA supports emerging designers and provides resources to help apparel brands create sustainable and ethical supply chains. Tara St. James is part of the BFDA Sustainable Strategies Lab and provides consulting services for designers in New York City. She is also the Production Coordinator and a research fellow with a specialty in zero-waste fashion design. Tara St. James shares her expertise based on fifteen years of

Figure 2: Designer Tara St James sewing in the Brooklyn Fashion Design Accelerator. (Photo by Sarah Kerens.)

Figure 3: Informative hangtag for Study NY's Conversations in Craft Sweatshirt. (Photo by Helen Trejo.)

managing global and local clothing supply chains. She teaches courses about sustainable textile sourcing, cut-and-sew fabric selection and negotiating with manufacturers at the BFDA.

MLJ Fashions in Manhattan, New York

Study NY manufactures clothing at MLJ Fashions in the New York City Fashion District. MLJ Fashions is approximately 30 years old and previously had a large factory in Brooklyn suitable for mass production. The factory closed during the 1990s and outsourced its large-scale production capabilities.

MLJ Fashions contributes to the contemporary NYC Fashion District by providing sample- and small-quantity production services. MLJ Fashions is critical to Study NY as a small business with limited edition production runs. The company employs six seamstresses. Study NY's 'Anti-Fashion Calendar' provides a consistent need for sewing services throughout the entire year rather than during peak seasons when sample production is in high demand.

Tara St James visits MLJ Fashions on a weekly basis as part of her commitment to supply-chain transparency. She explains the significance of supporting domestic clothing manufacturing:

> I want to support the job market here…I have more control over the production; it's a much faster lead time. I don't have to worry about shipping, or any problems with customs. So there's lots of benefits to producing here, but primarily it's because I want to support the local economy.

Study NY featured sample makers from MLJ Fashions in the 'Who Made My Clothes?' Fashion Revolution Day campaign in April 2015. It marked the two-year anniversary of the Rana Plaza factory collapse in Dhaka, Bangladesh, where 1,134 people died and thousands were injured (Clean Clothes Campaign 2015). Participation in the campaign conveys Study NY's commitment to supply-chain transparency, support for fair wages and ethical working conditions.

Farm-to-shelf retail

Study NY clothing is distributed to retail outlets throughout the United States, Canada, England, Denmark and Kuwait. Retailers pre-order Study NY clothing, which determines the quantity of styles produced. Tara St James explains, 'I'm only producing basically what's sold and a little bit extra for my own webshop. Which means I'm reducing a lot of excess inventory as well'. Study NY production is based on retailer and customer demand, rather than traditional supply, to meet anticipated customer demand.

The 'Conversations in Craft Sweatshirt' is made with Texas organic cotton. Study NY provides an informative narrative about the domestic supply chain. Artisanal embroidery features make each organic cotton sweatshirt unique.

To support artisanal crafts on a global scale, Study NY has sweatshirts embroidered in Peru and Afghanistan. Photographs of the embroidery design are distributed to artisans with a fixed dollar amount that indicates the labour and time expected for embroidering. Artisans receive instructions to stop embroidering once their labour matches the allocated dollar compensation. Since the wages are lower in Peru and Afghanistan, Study NY is able to provide more work hours for artisans. The final embroidery details reflect the unique geographies of production at local and global scales.

Study NY manages its own textile-waste supply chain. Organic cotton textile remnants are repurposed to create the 'Weaving Hand Sweatshirt'. Study NY commissions hand weaving to the Brooklyn Weavers Guild, and each sweatshirt is unique with slight variations based on the hand-cut fabric scraps and colour variation (Weaving Hand 2015).

Conclusion

The organic cotton supply chain of Study NY exemplifies the feasibility of domestic production in the twenty-first century. With awareness of the limited

Figure 4: Weaving Hand Sweatshirt made of upcycled cotton.
(Photo by Sacha Maric.)

supply of cotton as a water-thirsty fibre, Study NY also integrates alternative fibres such as linen, hemp, alpaca and wool. Tara St James's 'Uniform Collection' limited edition approach and the 'Anti-Fashion Calendar' align with slow fashion. It prompts attention to the value of the clothing and key contributors such as organic cotton farmers and sewers. The Texas Organic Cotton Marketing Cooperative provides a deeper layer of farm-to-fashion transparency by hosting an annual 'Fall Field Day' that allows designers, customers and the general pubic opportunities to meet farmers, as well as see the fields and cotton gin processing. The transparency of the Study NY supply chain gives greater social meaning to the final Study NY clothes, and is an example of a slow fashion brand.

Acknowledgements

Special thanks to Tara St James, Daniel Sanders, Kelly Pepper and Professor Tasha L. Lewis.

References

Clean Clothes Campaign (2015), 'Rana Plaza', http://www.clean-clothes.org/ranaplaza. Accessed 30 June 2015.

Myers, D. and Stolton, S. (eds) (1999), *Organic Cotton: From Field to Final Product*, London: Intermediate Technology Publications.

OTA (Organic Trade Association) (2015), '2013 and Preliminary 2014: U.S. Organic Cotton Production & Marketing Trends', http://ota.com/sites/default/files/indexed_files/2013%20 and%20 2014%20Organic%20Cotton%20Report.pdf. Accessed 30 June 2015.

Spiritex (2015), http://www.spiritex.net. Accessed 30 June 2015.

Study NY (2015), http://study-ny.com. Accessed 30 June 2015.

TOCMC (Texas Organic Cotton Marketing Cooperative) (2015), http://www.texasorganic.com. Accessed 30 June 2015.

Textile Exchange (2014), 'Life Cycle Assessment (LCA) of Organic Cotton: A Global Average', http://farmhub.textileexchange.org/upload/library/Farm%20reports/LCA_of_Organic_Cotton%20 Fiber-Summary_of%20Findings.pdf. Accessed 30 June 2015.

Textile Exchange (2015), 'Organic Cotton Market Report 2014 Overview', http://textileexchange.org/resource-center/reports-and-publications/2014-organic-cotton-report. Accessed 30 June 2015.

Wakelyn, P. and Chaudry, M. (2007), 'Organic Cotton', in S. Gordon and Y. Hsieh (eds), *Cotton: Science & Technology*, Cambridge: Woodhead Publishing in Textiles, pp. 130–75.

Weaving Hand (2015), http://weavinghand.org. Accessed 30 June 2015.

Notes

1 India produces 74 per cent of the global organic cotton yields (Organic Textile Exchange 2015). Syria is also a leading producer of organic cotton, but data collection was not possible due to the conflict at the time. Additional leading organic cotton countries are Burkina Faso, Egypt, Mali, Uganda and Peru (OTA 2015).

2 Organic cotton can only grow in specific areas. Key environmental factors are 'well drained soil, a long growing season, moderate rainfall and a late freeze that minimizes pests and defoliates the plants for harvest' (OTA 2015: 6).

3 Other fibres processed include Tencel, hemp and recycled cotton/polyester blends.

Raleigh Denim: Curating Each Detail to Create the Perfect Jeans

Stephen Guarino

Joseph H. Hancock, II

Introduction

Victor Lytvinenko and Sarah Yarborough started Raleigh Denim as a small project in their college apartment, but that small project has grown to establish retail locations in Raleigh, North Carolina, and New York City. Quality over quantity is the underlying principle of the Raleigh Workshop; with meticulous attention to even the most minuscule details, individual hands make every pair of its denim jeans with the utmost care.

Because cotton is one of the most prolific materials available domestically, sourcing materials from North Carolina was a simple decision for Lytvinenko and Yarborough. Driven by design and creativity, the pair sought to maintain quality by internally overseeing the production process and keeping it as geographically condensed as possible. As sustainability lies at the core of the company's values, it has minimized its carbon footprint by working with local farmers and mills. Raleigh Workshop uses denim from Cone Denim's White Oak plant in Greensboro, North Carolina, which is a mere eighty miles away. Using American Draper X3 fly shuttle looms and back to the 1940s White Oak produces high quality selvedge denim, adding to the character and integrity of Raleigh Workshop's jeans.

Lytvinenko and Yarborough have found unparalleled value in having employees who are familiar with more than just one part of the production process, keeping quality at a premium. So, unlike other factories, the production floor is staffed by about fifteen people, each being cross-trained on how to produce a complete pair of denim jeans. The factory is lined with authentic vintage sewing machines dating back to the early 1920s and 1930s, some of which add invaluable character to the garments. 'There are a few machines that do really beautiful stitches that you can't really recreate with new machines', Lytvinenko states. 'They're slower and old and finicky, but I think they give our jeans the character and quality that we're looking for'.

Each jean production process takes about three to four weeks on the production line, with the factory producing about 250 pairs of jeans per week. New patterns and designs are created daily, with minor adjustments made after every run; even a change in material requires pattern modifications. So, while one run of a particular fit might be in a raw denim using a particular weight, if the weight or starch amount is altered even slightly for the next run, the pattern essentially needs to be redesigned. Although alterations are made with every pair of jeans produced, entirely new designs are explored every season. Colour direction is loosely based on trend reports to ensure that it complements and mixes well with other products on the overall denim market.

Even more so than trends and current popular styles, Raleigh Workshop relies on the feedback and input of its peers and customers. The company has become the destination for the person who values quality and style, and for the people who care about story and process. For Raleigh Workshop, it is about portraying a message of authenticity. 'We try to be honest, transparent, real and accessible,' says Yarborough. 'We try to

Figure 1: Founders Sarah Yarborough and Victor Lytvinenko. (Photo Courtesy of Raleigh Denim.)

Figure 2: Victor Lytvinenko (Co-founder/Designer) and Chris Ellsberg (Pattern Maker). (Photo Courtesy of Raleigh Denim.)

Figure 3: The Reece Buttonhole Machine is just one of many vintage machines that are found at Raleigh Denim. (Photo Courtesy of Raleigh Denim.)

Figure 4: Worker using the cutting machine.
(Photo Courtesy of Raleigh Denim.)

Figure 5: The production process at Raleigh Denim. (Photo Courtesy of Raleigh Denim.)

Figure 6: The production process at Raleigh Denim. (Photo Courtesy of Raleigh Denim.)

remain active in our community, in the business, and in our lives – we think those things are important.'

Initially a company producing only men's denim, Raleigh Workshop has evolved into a full workshop and somewhat of a curatorial destination store. The original workshop, seated on the edge of town, unmarked, without any windows, left Lytvinenko and Yarborough with adventurous people who wanted to purchase jeans, but no actual retail store. After moving into a new location, the current 'curatory' was created with the intention of being a showroom, a place simply to display a few of the styles for people to look at or try on. The tiny showroom was perfect, but the wholesaling side of Raleigh Workshop quickly influenced the curatory as a retail space. Through travel, Lytvinenko and Yarborough would meet brands and designers with goods complementary to Raleigh Denim. Inspired by their stories and history, the pair decided it only made sense to begin stocking other products that they believed in and wanted to see continue in the world. And so the curatory was born, with every item a story to tell…

Stephen Guarino (SG): How did the jean project come about to begin with – that's not your average undertaking?

Sarah Yarborough (SY): Victor wanted some pants. It was cheap, but it wasn't easy. He had a pair of pants that were falling apart that he had gotten in Europe that had fit really well. They were kind of jean-ish – like a heavy twill material. At the time, the fits were very different so getting a durable, jean kind of pant here that was tailored and fit really well, sounds weird to say now, but it wasn't available and if it was, it was very high end, like Dior-ish, and we could not afford that in college. We were makers and doers and interested in process, so Victor started taking them apart to make a pattern from them to see if he could make a pair just because he wanted another pair similar. And then it kind of got out of control – snowballed.

SG: At what point did you guys realize that Raleigh Workshop could become a viable company?

Victor Lytvinvenko (VL): It was like the summer of 2007 when people started buying jeans from us while we were in our apartment. That's when we were like, wow people will actually pay us what it's worth to make these things. That's when we filed all the papers to become a business.

SG: Why is it important to manufacture everything in the United States, and in this case specifically, North Carolina?

SY: It felt right to us. Also, we built our own factory so that we could make things the way that we wanted to make them, so it was more driven by design and more driven by what we wanted to make, and we couldn't do that unless we did it here. It's in our control over the process from beginning to end, and the quality.

SG: Why do you think cotton might be preferred from a consumer standpoint?

SY: I think comfort, familiarity and understandability. It is something you can wrap your head around, you know where it comes from and there is a certain comfort in that and then it's also not itchy, it breathes, it is versatile – depending on the weave or the knit or whatever, you can do something kind of refined, you can do something kind of rugged.

SG: Why did you decide to keep everything in-house – distribution, production, manufacturing, retail, etc.?

SY: I think that is probably a series of decisions made in response to the opportunities or the situation. I am not sure that if we planned it out from square one, knowing how much we would grow, that that's the path we would choose – it does not mean it is a bad one; it

Figure 7: The retail space for Raleigh Denim at the curatory. (Photo Courtesy of Raleigh Denim.)

Figure 8: The New York City flagship store in Nolita. (Photo Courtesy of Raleigh Denim.)

is just like, if we have an opportunity to open a store, we look at everything, and OK, yeah, let us give that a try because that seems to make sense, and then some things are just determined by scale.

Right now we actually have a warehouse that we work with in New Jersey that helps us with distribution, but at the scale we are, we can handle it ourselves. We seem to benefit from having all that information, like knowing exactly what's in stock and being able to touch it and see it and that helps us. I think if we get much bigger, then we'll have to start delegating some things, but I think we've done a lot of learning by doing, which makes it hard to know what third party to hire or what resource to use until we've done it. We've learned a lot along the way, so some of those things are things that we're learning [and] we just haven't handed off yet.

SG: Going back to scale, do you think the business model is scalable? And what major changes do you see happening in order to grow and expand?

SY: The short answer is yes I think it is scalable. I think that down the line we may consider automating some parts of the process just because it's more efficient. Some parts of our process are just slow and difficult just because they're slow and difficult, not because the slow and difficult way necessarily adds a whole lot of value or character, but some of the slow and difficult things we do add a ton of value and character. So we may streamline some parts to make it a lot more scalable.

SG: How do plan to maintain the quality and integrity of the pieces? Is there anything you absolutely wouldn't change or stray from?

SY: I think that it's really important that everyone who works with us be cross-trained to some degree and not pigeonholed into one task. That's something that's important to us. Everyone doesn't need to know everything, but a lot of factories are set up so that one person does one operation and they just become really great at that operation. We like to have a little bit of variety in there so that people understand more than their

process, which keeps the quality high. If you're familiar with more parts than just your part, you can notice when something isn't exactly correct or up to par, and since everything is not automated, that keeps everyone engaged and keeps our quality really high. And I think that this will be interesting to see if this maintains, but my biggest thing would be to keep it made in the States, no matter what. I think that we can be really flexible within that parameter. That's just because this is where we live and we want to participate in the economy here as much as possible.

VL: That's what we feel like is right.

SG: Who is the ideal Raleigh Denim customer?

VL: Someone who cares about quality, who cares about style.

SY: I think the ideal customer is someone who is interested in story and process, someone who thinks about how the things they use in their life or the things that they enjoy in their life – products, experiences or whatever it may be – how those things came to be. So if you pick up your coffee mug and you love it because it is perfectly proportioned, and it keeps your coffee the right temperature and it like feels good in your hand and it is your favourite colour and it was made by a great designer, then you are our person.

SG: If you had to define your target customer, who is it?

SY: When we started, we were just men's and our target market was ages 28 to 45 or 50, probably Master's degree, of a certain income and, you know, Whole Foods shopper, but we've had kids in college that have saved up their summer-job money to come – I mean, we had one dude call his mom from the floor because they were ten dollars more than he thought and he wanted to make sure that was OK because he would be saving all summer. We have had multi-generational visits, like a grown man and then his father who used to work in the apparel industry, used to work at a mill or knew someone at Cone and was just so thrilled to see production in the States, you know, just some 75-year-old man like happily – so we have been really blown away by how a fairly large chunk of our customers are not who we targeted; so we have trouble answering that question because we certainly don't want to rule anyone out.

SG: For the buying process of the store, how do you discover new brands, new designers and items you'd like to stock?

SY: Usually through travel is how we find them, and then the story needs to be compelling. Usually there's like a historic element or something interesting about the creative process, like we carry a line of apothecary stuff called Santa Maria Novella and it is perfumes and hand-pressed soaps and stuff. It is made by a group of monks in a monastery in Italy; they have been making things since the 1300s using the same recipes. So things like that – tried and true and really fascinating. We usually stock things that are either a product or process that we want to see continue in the world. It makes me happy that that's happening, so that's something that I would want to carry.

SG: What was some of the thought behind the visual merchandising of the retail store?

SY: When we started that store, it was meant to just be a showroom, essentially. We used to be over in the warehouse on the edge of town, you know, in the back of the warehouse with no windows and low ceilings and it was just production. We didn't advertise, and it was in an unmarked building and people would come down there and shuffle into the back and be like, 'We wanted to get some pants.' And we are like, 'That is crazy. We do not actually sell them here but, you know, kudos to you for making the trip, so yeah let's work that out.' So when we moved here we thought we should have a little area where we had a few of the styles for people to either see what we did or try a few on, but it wasn't

meant to be a full-fledged store.

Since we have the wholesale side in addition to the retail side, we meet a lot of brands and designers that we respect and have complementary products, and it's like of course we should carry that – that would be awesome to bring back to Raleigh. So it sort of grew organically from that, but we had already built the store out in that tiny little shotgun area so there's only so much you can do with it. We knew we wanted some sort of connection between the store and production, so that's why there's the long window where you can see into things being made, but then everything else is a reflection of our style.

SG: How does the New York City store differ from what's going on here?

SY: The New York City store does not have production attached. It does have a hemming machine and we mark all the jeans to length for our customers and hem them, which is pretty fun. So there's still a little bit of action and a little bit of process, but it is also not as multi-branded as our store here. It is more our stuff and then accessories. Design-wise, it is different.

VL: Yeah, design-wise it is very forward-looking, whereas this one is more… I don't want to say *backwards-looking*, but it's more *comfortable*. The store in New York, it feels more like a gallery. It is a white metal wire frame that everything hangs off of. It is a lot more designed.

SG: What went into the design theory behind that?

SY: We worked with some wonderful, amazing architects. We worked with their New York office and went through iterations. They came down and visited here and talked about what we were looking for and what we do now and what we hope to do in the future and came up with like thirteen different schemes and this one seemed the most flexible. That was the thing that we landed on, that what we needed most was flexibility, so that we could clear the store out and have an event, or something that would lend itself well to stacks of jeans and maybe later a full collection and dresses or something. Things where we could highlight collaborations and exhibit, because that crossover is interesting to us. So this framework was the solution that we came up with. It divides the framework sort of into three sections: a foyer, a main area and a parlour. That idea was based on a traditional Southern home, so the deeper you get the more intimate it is. And so that spatial idea and materially this framework that would allow us to attach things to it or take them off, but those were the basis for the design.

SG: Where do your efforts lie in terms of sustainability?

VL: It is part of our mission to be as economically, socially and environmentally sustainable as we can at any given point and it's a very grey area, especially depending on the size of the company. If it is sent to the cotton gin, the spinning mill, the weaving mill and then to us all within a couple hundred miles, we have been able to reduce our carbon footprint to a very, very, very small number. We worked with a couple of farmers in North Carolina recently to grow the first crop of certified organic cotton ever grown in North Carolina, so not only did it have one of the smallest carbon footprints, it was also the first crop of certified organic – and that is continuing to grow. We have been a part of a group of businesses buying this cotton and it's been growing year after year pretty well. So those are the two main points on the environmental side and those things also lead into the kind of socially and economically sustainable points in supporting our local economies in having manufacturing nearby.

SY: We also encourage people not to wash their jeans much, which is a small thing but it really adds up. Americans overwash their clothes all the time. And we also love it when people have eleven pairs, and some people do, but we think it's really awesome whether it's our garment or not. We're proponents of buying one wonderful thing instead of four OK things. That's something we live by; it's something we encourage.

VL: Quality over quantity.

SG: Quality over quantity is a big risk – are there any factors that you think were particularly key to your success as a company?

VL: The timing was really important. We didn't know it at the time but looking back we were, I believe, one of the early champions of quality over quantity with an artisanal process and in-house production and educating the public about all of that. I mean, we learned shortly before we started this what selvedge denim was and what raw denim was and we visited Cone and we learned about that and were like, oh my God, what an amazing resource.

SY: Yeah, proximity was an important one. So yeah, proximity and timing. But when we started talking to customers about that, they had no idea that selvedge denim was new, raw denim was new, something made entirely here was new, and focusing on those things was a new angle, so I think that we were fortunate to be at the beginning of that. I think the other thing is just accessibility; people love coming in here and seeing things moving. I think to you and me that is not novel, but most of the world doesn't see how things are made, and if they do it is on a much larger scale or much smaller scale.

VL: I think most of the people that come into our shop have never seen a sewing factory. So I think we owe a lot of our success to the fact that people are just interested because it's visible.

SG: What have some of your biggest challenges and successes been?

SY: I think our biggest success is to be here right now.

And in terms of accomplishment-type successes, I would say being accepted into the CFDA […] because they've been an amazing resource for us. It's an organization that you're voted in by your peers, so for other people in the industry to say, 'We think what you're doing is valuable and we'd like to be connected so we can all help each other continue to do things like that' – that's huge. That takes the competition out of things and opens a lot of doors, so I'm really grateful for that.

Biggest challenges, I think the broad one for me would be balancing creative time and necessary development. We need to be thinking in new ways and we need to be having a little fun and innovating and pushing forward design-wise, balancing the need and want for that with the logistics of running a business, which are very office-oriented, very cashflow-oriented, very management-oriented, which we enjoy much of the time, but sometimes it's just freaking hard. So that is my biggest challenge. Then you can break that down into like 8 million smaller ones.

VL: Yeah the biggest challenge has changed year to year.

We have a biggest challenge, we dig in, we figure it out, we move on, we grow a little, something changes and there is an entirely different biggest challenge, but you go with it, you move on, it is a continual thing. I feel like people dream that they're going to get to a place where it is not necessarily easy but the systems work and we don't need to invent new systems again for the fifth time for the fifth year in a row and things will stick.

SG: What motivates you?

SY: I want things to be perfect and they never are, ever.

VL: I'm motivated to build a product that we're really proud of and do something that's not been done, essentially, and to have an impact, both in our market and also locally in our community. Be a positive force.

Figure 9: Raleigh Denim. (Photo Courtesy of Raleigh Denim.)

Figure 10: Raleigh Denim. (Photo Courtesy of Raleigh Denim.)

Figure 11: Founders Sarah Yarborough and Victor Lytvinenko. (Photo Courtesy of Raleigh Denim.)

How the Oranges Allowed Lilly to Blossom from Juices to Dresses

Shahidah Hasan
Nioka N. Wyatt

Figure 1: Lilly Pulitzer in her retail store in Palm Beach, Florida. (Photo Courtesy of lillypulitzer.com.)

History

The shift dress was the catalyst that allowed Lilly Pulitzer's brand to evolve from a bright and colourful cotton smock designed to hide juice stains to a leader in the fashion industry. Lilly wanted a way to mask the juice stains and look fashionable while working at her juice stand in Palm Beach. More than fifty years later, the popular shift has revolutionized women's style of dress, promoted the use of cotton garments for women, and developed a culture of women wearing pink adorned with prints. The brand is a symbol of femininity, classic silhouettes with a twist, and embraces the shift from girlhood to womanhood. The products are popular with mothers and socialites who seek versatility and cotton luxury. Within every Lilly print, you can identify the brand's logo through decadent shoe horses, seashells, starfish, palm trees and oranges; all the essentials that pay homage to where her company developed. Since the 1950s, the simple, nourishing ingredient of oranges has been the fruit of the company's success, and continues to be a significant visual element in her retail operations.

How the oranges allowed Lilly to blossom

The initial stages of Lilly's design talent began when she purchased fabric at Woolworth and paid her seamstress to develop the products. The dress became extremely popular with the customers, so Lilly transitioned her business model from selling juices to selling dresses. With the help of First Lady Jacqueline Kennedy, who

Figure 2: Lilly Pulitzer collection. (Photo Courtesy of lillypulizter.com.)

was seen wearing one of the dresses on vacation, the Lilly shift became iconic.

Lilly Pulitzer's first designs were similar to the shift; however, there were slight variations made to the neckline, length, darts and slits to add minute changes in each line. The high-society crowd loved her designs and business was strong for many years. After a quarter of a century in the business, Lilly went bankrupt.

For almost ten years, Lilly customers could only add to their collection if they purchased an item at a thrift shop or rummage sale. In 1993, two Philadelphians contacted Ms Pulitzer with aspirations to revive the brand. James B. 'Brad' Bradbeer, Jr, and Scott A. Beau-mont both Harvard M.B.A's formed Sugartown Worldwide. Inc. The company was founded in 1993 and is based in King of Prussia, Pennsylvania. Sugartown Worldwide, Inc. purchased the rights to the 'Lilly' name, but Lilly Pulitzer served as a creative consultant. James Bradbeer's mother, Sissy Bradbeer, worked in one of the Pulitzer shops in California and had a natural connection with the brand. James wore Lilly so much that he admits to being a 'big-time Lilly child'.

Doing business as Lilly Pulitzer, Sugartown Worldwide, Inc., developed a chain of apparel and accessories retail stores. When Sugartown relaunched Lilly products, it offered a wide variety of apparel and accessories for men, women and children. The company also provided bags, baubles, footwear and online gift cards. Sugartown's savvy business skills revitalized the brand and ensured that the Lilly customer was aware of the brand's new strategy and started selling products in boutiques and high-priced department stores like Neiman Marcus, Saks Fifth Avenue and Nordstrom. In lieu of operating in over thirty states, the products are also sold through the brand's e-commerce platform.

In December 2010, Sugartown Worldwide, Inc. operated as a subsidiary of Oxford Industries, Inc. Oxford paid $60 million for Sugartown Worldwide, Lilly Pulitzer's parent company. The deal noted that if the sales from Lilly reached a targeted earning, Oxford would pay up to $20 million in additional payments. Oxford expected the new purchase to contribute more than $75 million in sales, $11 million in operating income and 40¢ a share in profits for its 2011 fiscal year. Oxford Industries, Inc. is a global apparel company that designs, sources, markets and distributes products bearing the trademarks of the company-owned lifestyle brands as well as certain license and private-label apparel products. The company distributes its company-owned, lifestyle-branded products through its direct-to-consumer channel consisting of owned retail stores, e-commerce sites, and its wholesale distribution channel which includes better department stores and specialty stores. The company's business is primarily operated through four of its private labels, each with its own group of demographics. After being acquired by Oxford, the decision was made to no longer produce menswear since Tommy Bahama is one of Oxford's major menswear brands.

Company structure

Oxford Industries owns the company; however, Scott Beaumont, CEO, and James Bradbeer, Jr, President, operate Lilly and are listed as Management Executives under Oxford Industries. The corporate office, located in King of Prussia, Pennsylvania, is known as the Pink Palace. The majority of the business units are located at this corporate resort-style office with the exception of sales. The flagship store on the East Coast with the majority of foot traffic is located in the King of Prussia Mall in Pennsylvania, while the locations in Florida generate the most revenue for Lilly. The corporate culture at Lilly is a reflection of its strong brand image and of Lilly's mantra to have fun along the way. The Lilly team members work hard, but they also play hard at their after-work mixers on Fridays. The employees mirror the culture and brand positioning of Lilly's attire, and the message is evoked throughout the building. The employees embrace the freedom of working in an environment similar to a resort while cultivating relationships in Asia and collaborating on new lines and projects. The shades of pink, the palm trees, the intricate staircase, and images of Lilly with celebrities, family and close friends are featured throughout the Pink Palace.

One of Lilly's founding principles is to integrate continuous educational platforms for employees. In the beginning of her journey, Lilly worked with her friends to market the brand. If their husbands were working and they were at home, she supported the women through employment by opening stores and developing a sales team. Lilly was not only a designer, but also a mentor for many women. Cotton Incorporated offers educational workshops for industry representatives to build their knowledge and learn the latest developments in cotton. Similar to Lilly, the organization serves as a mentor and partner to leading firms that integrate cotton throughout their supply chain. Lilly Pulitzer encourages its employees to attend its seminars in New York or visit its headquarters in Cary, North Carolina. The company suggests that young leaders entering the field of fashion embrace being lifelong learners and engage in networking opportunities locally and globally.

Design and development

For a company that uses mainly colourful and fun tropical patterns, it is important for the designers to research sources of inspiration. It is integral to maintain freedom of expression while designing such intricate, mandated prints to eliminate pattern diffusion. Nonetheless, it is supported that employees take breaks to rest, relax and regroup. One of the strategies to maximize their creativity is for the designers to travel to festivals and islands such as Ibiza to gain inspiration. An integral part of the design process is to create a hidden 'Lilly' on each handcrafted item. This signature design element is the hallmark of an authentic Lilly Pulitzer design.

The design process at Lilly begins with an inspiration board while developing an array of colour inspirations, selecting cotton-inspired materials and creating miniature sketches of the garments. The designers create their palettes and select matching colour swatches, and the process of colour production begins. Lilly's colour department is responsible for selecting lab dips and strike offs for its collection. Lab dips are an assortment of colour variations for your materials. When lab dips are not within a certain parameter of the original colour, the colour may be rejected. Strike offs are replicas of your printed fabric and are also rejected if they are not within the standards and specifications that the company mandates. The initial samples are distributed through a courier service and further communication is conducted through e-mails with the mills throughout Hong Kong, China. Because Lilly's clothes are based on bright colours and bold prints, creating the perfect colour match is just as important as the design when working in the studio. Testing the materials and implementing strict quality-assurance guidelines are core principles at Lilly Pulitzer.

The company has a tradition in which the design team goes to the company's condominium in Palm Beach, Florida, for an all-night brainstorming session to evaluate and critique the upcoming lines. With CAD prints and paper dolls pinned to a merchandising board, the team works all night to further develop the collection. During this process, samples are reviewed from the factory and the entire line is reviewed in detail, focusing on key garments that exemplify the Lilly customer. Design collaborates with the merchandising team, whose primary function is selecting the style and identifying the number of units for production. The Business Analyst handles the projections by studying historical sales data and projections of past and future sales. The company's strategy is to focus on successful silhouettes while making minor changes to the neckline, hemline and design.

Since Lilly's inception, prints have been at the forefront of its design philosophy and in some cases appeal to both the 'Mother and Child'. The concept is not intentional at Lilly, but some of the prints have a high degree of popularity with both target markets. According to Linda Iem, Technical Designer at Lilly Pulitzer,

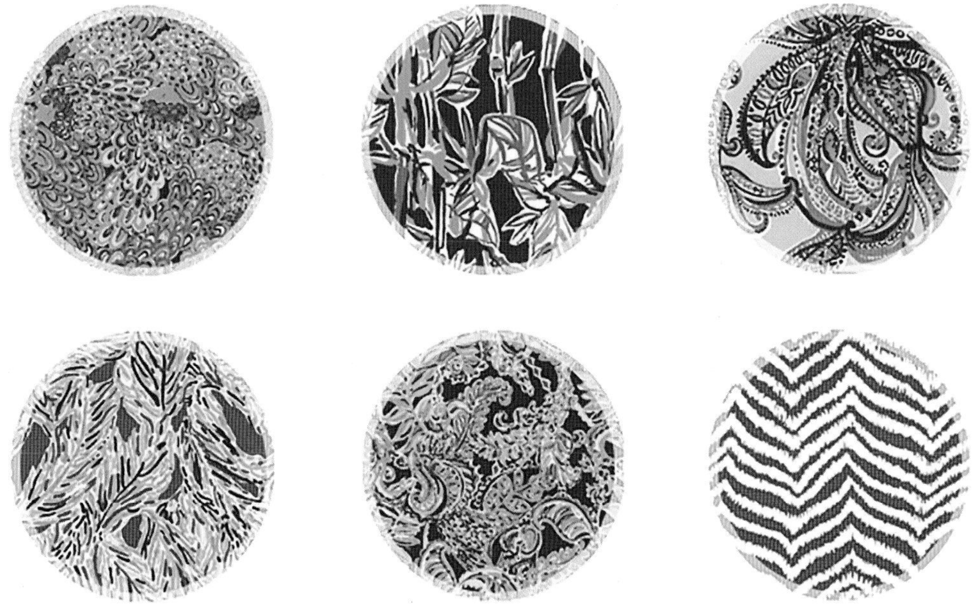

Figure 3: Print collection (from left to right): Lilly's Lagoon, Bamboom, Keep It Current, Palm Reader, Toucan Play and Zebron. (Photo Courtesy of lillypulitzer.com.)

Figure 4: Print collection (from left to right): Summer Haze, Casa Marina, Seaesta, Green Parrot and See And Be Seen. (Photo Courtesy of lillypulizter. com.)

Figure 5: Design studio at Lilly's corporate headquarters. (Photo by Nioka N. Wyatt.)

Figure 6: Lilly pillows for Target. (Photo Courtesy of pinterest.com.)

'If there is a style that does particularly well, design will try to develop a similar style for their younger consumers to maximize sales'.

Target collaboration

Did Lilly Pulitzer facilitate the collaboration with its Target counterpart?

Target Corporation was founded in Roseville, Minnesota, in 1962 by George Draper Dayton. In May 2015, Target Corporation reported over $72 billion in revenue. The company offers a wide assortment of products developed through private-label merchandise and exclusive brands. In the past, Target has collaborated with high-end designers such as Jason Wu and Missoni. Target wanted to extend its winning streak of high-profile designer collaborations with the 250-piece Lilly Pulitzer collection. The idea for this collaboration was about offering the Target customers a collection that embraced colour, print and pattern in a bold, refreshing way. Target viewed Lilly Pulitzer as the perfect company to develop this collection, given the brand's inspiring heritage with print, pattern and resort aesthetic.

Although Target was responsible for the majority of the project, only a few key individuals from Lilly's design and marketing team were involved with the development of fifteen prints for the collection. The prints were designed and developed by Lilly and were only produced for this collaboration. The goal was to gain a broader audience while bringing customers to the stores, but not to oversaturate the market. The collection included clothing as well as curvy sizes, shoes, accessories and home decor ranging in price from $2 to $150. The collaboration was Lilly's first venture into outdoor decor, beach accessories and bar items. Although some customers were left empty-handed, the project served the purpose to generate additional eyeballs and buzz, as well as fuel innovation, add products to Target's eclectic mix and foster collaboration..

Marketing

Lilly has a well-established customer base that is devoted to its resort-chic styles and silhouettes. Each year, eager customers await the annual sale at Lilly Pulitzer's distribution centre. Savvy customers travel from all over the world to buy products at a discounted rate of approximately 70 per cent off the retail value, which includes accessories, shoes and gifts. Lilly's employees organize the sample sales and the majority of the items sold are one-of-a-kind garments that are not produced. The 2015 sale generated the highest revenue in the history of the sample sale. The staff at Lilly attributes the high sales to the collaboration with Target that occurred prior to the annual sale.

Target utilized technology to promote the collaboration with Lilly Pulitzer. The retailer created its first app for the launch in stores. The week before the launch, a digital and social media campaign was implemented. Print ads were running in April magazines that featured some of the exclusive Lilly Pulitzer prints from the collaboration, but not the actual products. Since Lilly Pulitzer is in a niche market, it is extremely selective when committing to partnerships; however, this collaboration was a win-win situation. This collaboration was Target's largest designer collaboration to date. While Target serves as one of the world's largest retailers in the United States, it facilitated the collaboration with Lilly Pulitzer.

The pop-up shop at Bryant Park Grill was more of a team effort between Target and Lilly Pulitzer. The pop-up shop opened a few days before the in-store launch and featured male counterparts in formal attire serving drinks. About 500 to 600 people were waiting outside at eight o'clock in the morning when the doors opened. Shoppers at the pop-up were limited to five items to make the collection available to as many as possible and to avoid people making bulk purchases, which sometimes leads to products being sold on eBay. The 250 items for sale at both the pop-up and in-store launch sold out quickly. The collaboration with Target

Figure 7: Lilly for Target promotional campaign in Bryant Park. (Photo Courtesy of pinterest.com.)

Figure 8: Lilly's Octopus print. (Photo by Linda Iem.)

was not the first time that Lilly had allowed its exclusive prints to be used for limited edition styles.

Opportunities for growth and development

Lilly goes through the design process for four seasons a year. Each season begins with it approximately 100 styles, and only half of those products are manufactured. The company develops a vast number of samples and the process for design and development takes around 24 months to complete. Over the years, the company has made improvements to reduce its timeframe by implementing technological systems to extract and compile data that the company can use to make real-time business decisions. The company is very focused on reducing supply-chain lead-time, becoming leaner, more efficient and more cost effective. With technology playing such a vital role in the shopping experience for customers, it is imperative that retailers make all transactions easy and convenient. In early 2015, Lilly Pulitzer implemented new Point-of-Sale (POS), Store Inventory Management and Tablet Retailing applications. Lilly Pulitzer will also implement a Warehouse Management System (WMS) to enhance warehouse operations with the hopes of a measurable return on investment. These changes will make products seamlessly available to customers through any channel they select. One of the major advantages of Lilly Pulitzer implementing a WMS system is the location of its distribution centre. These systems require a significant amount of training and trials; however, the distribution centre is in close proximity to the Pink Palace – a key metric in launching new platforms.

Lilly Pulitzer's brand was known as unconventional, whimsical and bold-faced pink. She candidly admitted that she was clueless about business; however, she still wears the crown for demonstrating passion, turning palms into prints, commercializing pink and *shifting* her orange stand into a juicy dress business.

References

Anon. (n.d.), 'History & Heritage of Lilly Pulitzer: Lilly Pulitzer', *History & Heritage of Lilly Pulitzer: Lilly Pulitzer*, https://www.lillypulitzer.com/content.jsp?pageName=heritage. Accessed 21 June 2015.

Anon. (2015), 'Lilly Pulitzer Puts Customers First with Manhattan Associates Technology', *Lilly Pulitzer Puts Customers First with Manhattan Associates Technology*, 14 May. Accessed 21 May 2015.

Anon. (2015), 'Target, Pulitzer Tandem Gets App', *WWD: Women's Wear Daily*, 209: 68, pp. 9–10.

Bogaert, Pauline Pinard (1994), 'Blossoming Again: The Look of Lilly Pulitzer, Who Set Society On Fire Years Ago with Her Bold Print Dresses, Is Back, Thanks to Three Philadelphians with Fond Memories', *Philly*, 21 August, http://articles.philly.com/1994-08-21/living/25841508_1_sugartown-worldwide-lilly-pulitzer-nancy-gary. Accessed 1 August 2015.

de la Merced, Michael J. (2010), 'Prep Stays Hot as Lilly Pulitzer Is Sold for $60 Million', *NY Times*, 21 December, http://dealbook.nytimes.com/2010/12/21/prep-stays-hot-as-lilly-pulitzer-is-sold-for-60-million/. Accessed 19 June 2015.

Mosendz, Polly (2015), 'The Cult of Lilly Pulitzer', *Newsweek Global*, 164: 19, pp. 58–60.

Pederson, Jay P. (ed.) (2011), 'Target Corporation', *International Directory of Company Histories*, vol. 122, Detroit: St. James Press.

Speer, Jordan K. (2004), 'Color Profile: Examining Processes at Lilly® PULITZER', *Apparel*, 45: 10, pp. 22, 24, 26.

Figure 1: Eileen Fisher collection, Autumn/Winter 2015. (Photo by Autumn S. Newell.)

Introduction

Since the beginning, Eileen Fisher created her name-sake brand with a strong commitment to incorporating social consciousness, sustainability, health and well-being into its corporate culture and products. The company was built to reflect her own personal desire for simple, timeless clothing made from high quality fabrics that could be worn together. Original designs were made exclusively of natural fibres, with cotton and linen being Eileen's favourites. The brand's design philosophy and corporate culture has always been a reflection of Eileen's belief that her products and business can be a force for positive change, particularly for women in the world.

Eileen Fisher company background

Eileen Fisher founded her company in 1984 with $350 and an idea to create comfortable clothing for women that could accommodate function and allow the wearer to express her style with elegance and ease. Today, the company has grown immensely with over $430 million in annual revenue and 67 Eileen Fisher stores across the United States, Canada and in London. The core values of the company are imbedded in the design of the products and the business model.

After over 30 years, Fisher has continued to work and be involved with design, company operations and the overall vision for the brand, but believes in incorporating the passions and interests of her employees to enhance the impact of the brand. Employees are encouraged to collaborate and use their roles to make a difference for environmental and human rights issues within the company's global supply chain. Fisher herself has always been very passionate about women's issues and established the Eileen Fisher Community Foundation as an extension of her mission to promote leadership among women and girls.

Role of cotton at Eileen Fisher

Eileen Fisher as a brand was founded around the use of natural fibres, using only cotton, linen, silk and wool in its original designs. During its three decades in business, the company has expanded the fibers used in designs by adding synthetics such as rayon, viscose and Tencel, as well as some natural–synthetic blends to enhance the comfort and performance of its garments. However, cotton has always been a staple for the brand, making up about 20 per cent of the total product line and often included in the contents of the blended-fibre fabrics. Cotton remains a prominent fabric choice for the brand, not only because it was one of Eileen's original favourites but also because Eileen Fisher customers request cotton products throughout the year. Even during the winter season, customers desire cotton for not only its feel but also because many customers experience sensitivity to fibres like wool that are used in collections for colder months.

Eileen Fisher believes in developing a familiarity with the fabrics used in collections. It repeats a set of core fabrics each season in order to allow designers the opportunity for reinvention and for the customer to build new looks into their wardrobes. One example of these core fabrics is organic cotton jersey, which typically consists of 90–100 per cent organic cotton but can also be blended with viscose or spandex. Organic cotton jersey has appeared in each collection since 2004, when the brand decided to incorporate it into the design of its yoga apparel. Organic cotton is used across product lines, particularly in summer months, and is included in the design of sweaters, tanks, T-shirts, jackets, skirts, dresses, leggings, denim products and more. The organic cotton jersey pieces are manufactured in the United States as part of the brand's commitment to maintaining a percentage of its production domestically.

Sustainability and cotton production

As part of Eileen Fisher's commitment to environmental sustainability, the brand has continuously expanded its use of organic cotton since first using it in 2004 and maintains a strong commitment to choosing and supporting the organic cotton farming industry. Currently, the company uses organic cotton for the vast majority of its cotton products and hopes to use exclusively 100 per cent organic cotton and linen fibres by the year 2020 as part of its Vision 2020 mission.

Eileen Fisher's organic cotton is typically sourced from the world's top-five organic cotton producing countries including China, India, the United States, Peru and Turkey. In 'The 17,000-mile Yoga Tank', on the Eileen Fisher website, the story of a transparent global chain starts with a small farmer in Arizona who grows a special type of long-staple organic cotton from heritage seeds that have never been genetically modified. The cotton is then sent to a yarn spinner in Senhoff, Switzerland, who is one of the only spinners in the world – none exist in the United States – that possesses both the expertise to work with extra-long-staple organic cotton fibres and the capability of adhering to strict Global Organic Textile Standards (GOTS) that meet organic certification requirements. From Switzerland, the yarns make their way to Montreal where they are transformed into a stretch-knit fabric and custom dyed with colours for the season before being shipped back to the New York City area. Once arriving back in the United States, the fabric is transformed by one of Eileen Fisher's three New York City manufacturing partners by being cut and sewn into organic cotton jersey products.

As a strong supporter of organic cotton, the Eileen Fisher company has been involved with the Organic Cotton Round Table created by the Textile Exchange, which supports research activities around the state of non-GMO seed supplies and requirements for the success of this sector within the cotton market (Barrie 2014). A number of sustainable cotton farming options exist outside of organic cotton, but the system of accountability and certification available through organic cotton provides a secured sense of transparency and integrity within Eileen Fisher's production supply chain.

Domestic manufacturing

Domestic manufacturing is another important aspect of the company's DNA. When the company was founded in the 1980s, it was able to produce all its clothing in New York City. Since the early 1990s, that option has changed dramatically as domestic manufacturing has seen significant off-shoring to mostly Asian nations, with China emerging as the dominant producer. Over the past two decades, as Eileen Fisher has seen the most growth and increased production, the brand has partnered with international manufacturers. The majority of its manufacturing takes place in China, Turkey and Peru. However, despite industry norms, the brand continues to manufacture a strong 20 per cent of Eileen Fisher products in US factories. Products produced in the United States include both cut-and-sew knits, like the organic cotton jersey line produced in New York City, and woven garments such as organic cotton denim produced in a Los Angeles factory.

The company believes that developing and supporting strong relationships with apparel manufacturers is a key aspect of both maintaining and reviving US industry. However, because apparel manufacturing has been on the decline for the past two and a half decades, much of the expertise and infrastructure no longer exists in the United States. In response, Eileen Fisher has invested heavily in domestic production contractors. As a part of its commitment, the brand regularly visits domestic production facilities. The brand has invested in safety and workers'-rights training as well as production education and skill-building initiatives to maintain the level of garment quality that Eileen Fisher customers have come to expect. In turn, US manufacturing partners also keep core fabrics on hand as a way to support production and make a commitment to future orders. Although the company places importance on maintaining and developing a large percentage of its manufacturing in the United States, it acknowledges that, more often than not, global commodities are combined to create its goods. The organic cotton jersey products begin with the cotton farmer in Arizona and are eventually assembled in the United States, but the labelling states that they are made of imported fabrics in the United States, because the fibre must travel the globe to become the fabric used in the garment.

Producers of Eileen Fisher garments must comply with SA8000 standards, which were developed in 1997 by Social Accountability International (SAI) in response to the sweatshop scandals in association with outsourced apparel manufacturing. While not all of Eileen Fisher's producers are officially SA8000 certified, it does use third-party auditors to verify that all of its manufacturers are compliant with established labour and health standards.

Challenges, successes and the future of Eileen Fisher

As a company, Eileen Fisher actively works to improve its position and environmental impact in areas of fibre and fabric production, selection and dyeing, as well as human rights issues throughout its global supply chain. Megan Meiklejohn, Eileen Fisher's Supply Chain Transparency Specialist, works to map out the brand's supply chains through every stage of the process, from farm to finished product. One of the goals behind mapping the supply chain is to understand how far a product has to travel around the globe until completion. Understanding this allows the brand to evaluate the efficiency of its supply chain and seek ways to reduce the carbon footprint of its materials and garments.

In 2013, the brand began taking on sustainability in a whole new way by incorporating the concept of 'systems thinking' into its approach to environmental and human rights issues. A group was assembled called the Sustainable Design Team, comprised of employees who represent stakeholders in each aspect of the company's supply chain, including leaders from design, manufacturing and inventory, as well as a consumer representative. Together, the team came up with what they call Vision 2020, comprised of specific goals for sustainability that embody the values of the brand. The Vision is comprised of goals around six key issues: fibre

Figure 2: Organic cotton denim ready for production in Los Angeles factory. (Photo by Eileen Fisher.)

sourcing, fabric dyeing, planetary boundaries of resources, production impact on people, mapping global supply chains and end-of-life reuse. Along with Vision 2020, the company rolled out its No Excuses ad campaign that promoted products while also acknowledging the brand's successes, shortcomings and aspirations for the future. Eileen Fisher is also one of the few brands in the fashion industry practising extended producer responsibility for the products it creates and distributes, with its own unique model for supporting philanthropic activity that the brand's founder and namesake is so passionate about. The brand has experienced great success with its take-back programme, where Eileen Fisher-brand items can be returned to the company's retail locations in exchange for $5 in Recycling Rewards, which can be used towards their next purchase. The programme has taken back over 260,000 Eileen Fisher garments since its inception in 2009. Items are then sorted in-house and sold as 'Green Eileen' products in select stores around the country. Director of Sustainability Shona Quinn states that the company has so many end-of-life options for clothing, which brings huge potential to the Vision 2020 plan.

References

Barrie, L. (2014), 'Organic Cotton Faces Potential Supply Shortage', http://www.just style.com/analysis/spotlight-onorganic-cotton-faces-potential-supply-shortage_id122512.aspx. Accessed 23 February 2015.

Bloomberg (2014), 'Eileen Fisher: How Did I Get Here?', 11 December, http://www.bloomberg.com/bw/articles/2014-12-11/eileen-fisher-how-did-i-get-here. Accessed 4 June 2015.

Eileen Fisher (2015), 'Behind the Label', *Eileen Fisher,* http://www.eileenfisher.com/EileenFisher/Behind_the_Label/Behind_the_Label/Made_in_USA.jsp?bmLocale=en_US. Accessed 22 May 2015.

Eileen Fisher Ampersand (2015), http://eileenfisherampersand.com/. Accessed 24 May 2015.

Reference for Business (2015), 'Eileen Fisher Inc. – Company Profile, Information, Business Description, History, Background Information on Eileen Fisher Inc.', http://www.referenceforbusiness.com/history2/49/Eileen-Fisher-Inc.html. Accessed 22 February 2015.

Transforming trends is the ability to capture the essence of culture, connectivity and consumer insights into developing future generations of fashion products. Technological resources allow us to connect, share and like products throughout global markets at lightning speed. Trend forecasters can stream live fashion shows, travel the world and engage in the study of ethnography. The process of studying cultures, watching people and evaluating the economic and political genres of the world of fashion is defined as forecasting. Fashion centres in New York, London, Paris, Milan and Tokyo are recognized as premiere epicentres of depicting the next wave of fashion products.

Cultural geographer David Gilbert noted that this complex relationship underpins contemporary understandings of global fashion as a system orchestrated around a shifting network of world cities, particularly Paris, New York, London, Milan and Tokyo, but also incorporating (at various times) Moscow, Vienna, Berlin, São Paulo, Kuwait City, Cape Town, Barcelona, Antwerp, Delhi, Melbourne, Sydney, Shanghai, Hong Kong, Mumbai and others (Breward 2010).

Figure 1: Galleria Vittorio Emanuele II in Milan, Italy, is one of the oldest malls in the world. (Photo by Nioka N. Wyatt.)

Figure 2: Mobility of fashion in the twenty-first century. (Photo by Alicia Pinckney.)

Figure 3: Lockers and notions for inspiration.
(Photo by Alicia Pinckney.)

Jackson, Crang and Dwyer's (2004) study of the complexities of diasporic and transnational fashion cultures highlights more general ways that major cities have drawn upon their privileged positions in wider networks. Fashion in such centres has been shaped by flows of people (as cheap skilled labour, designers, entrepreneurs and consumers), materials, capital and ideas.

Today, we must shift our focus to Shanghai to think about the possibilities for fashion's world cities in the twenty-first century. China's growing region possesses not only huge manufacturing capacity, but also the largest emerging market and connoisseurs of luxury products. Shanghai's position in one of the main manufacturing regions of the country suggests parallels with the transformation of Milan in the 1970s and 1980s (Gilbert and Breward 2011).

Notable organizations such as Cotton Incorporated depict trends by studying global influences, reviewing historical artefacts, researching colours and materials, while analysing the ever-changing lifestyle of consumers. Cotton Incorporated's advisory team of forecasters blend social progressions and street styles to create the most innovative and informative analysis of trend progressions to its clients. Cotton Incorporated's expert team, Trend Forecasters, travels to the far corners of the world to research cotton trends and assess the creative landscape in lifestyle, fashion and product direction for major brands, retailers and textile mills.

Worth Global Style Network (WGSN) currently operates as a system of remote information sources. WGSN is still rooted in major fashion centres, with locations in London, New York, Milan, Paris, São Paulo, Hong Kong and Tokyo. Yet, the network has the potential to circumvent traditional fashion collections and shows, and to orchestrate simultaneous international launches of collections online. Since its inception, Fashion Snoops has partnered with leading fashion companies, organizations, trade associations and fabric companies to respond quickly to cultural shifts and market trends. The company's guiding principle is 'to bring clarity to what's next'. Fashion Snoops's innovative creative platform offers its clients real-time trend movements by providing the intersection of style, technology, art and leading fashion concepts. The site is equipped for mapping the evolution of various trends, which allows clients to link historical context with current applications of studying street styles from around the globe.

While many organizations are known for providing trend innovation in material and product development, Pantone infuses the art and science of developing colour stories throughout the apparel, automotive, home and interiors, and beauty industries. The Pantone book of colour encompasses an array of colours that serves as a starting point for designers and merchandisers in the global fashion ecosystem enabling them to select colours that are appropriate for their line and collection of merchandise. Leading colourific engineers that forecast the next generation of colours develop Pantone's formulas, colour standards and samples for clients. The company believes that, 'colour is the catalyst that sparks the sale, defines the space, and creates the magic and the mood for consumers'. Whether it is minion yellow, celosia orange, radiant orchid or cayenne, the equilibrium of colours can be identified on the colour wheel.

Throughout recent travels to major fashion cities, street styles were captured to depict the flavour of fashion, mainly in Milan and Venice, Italy. The Italians are known to demonstrate their impeccable taste in textile development and finely finished tailored garments. For this apparent reason, a trend study was conducted on Henry Cotton, which is a perfect fit to showcase how brands change the fabric and texture of lives.

The Henry Cotton store in Venice, Italy, infused similar trends identified on the Cotton Incorporated 'Trendcasters' forum. Sir Henry Cotton was a British golfer who was known for his eclectic style of dress inspired by the fashion evolution of the 1930s and 1940s. At the age of 19, he attended Langley Park and became the youngest head professional in the golf arena. He was an ultimate sportsman who also played rugby, cricket and tennis. In addition, he was an affluent trendsetter and avid business professional. Today, Henry Cotton has locations in Venice and Milan, Italy, and two locations in Seoul. The brand incorporates cotton products that are comfortable, and integrates cotton

Figure 4: Rocker chic Asians at Corso Como, in Milan, Italy. (Photo by Nioka N. Wyatt.)

Figure 5: Sustaining form and fashion while cycling. (Photo by Nioka N. Wyatt.)

Figure 6: Denim street style at Corso Como in Milan, Italy. (Photo by Nioka N. Wyatt.)

Figure 7: Provocative plaids. (Photo by Alicia Pinckney.)

Figure 8: Message Trend Products Nomination 'to give name' retail store Venice, Italy (Photo by Nioka Wyatt)

Figure 9: Colours of the Venetian Canals in Venice, Italy. (Photo by Nioka N. Wyatt.)

Figure 10: Global Sustainable Practices in Venice, Italy (Photo by Nioka Wyatt)

Figure 11: Henry Cotton window display in Venice, Italy. (Photo by Nioka N. Wyatt.)

Figure 12: Henry Cotton collection, Spring/Summer 2015. (Photo by Henry Cotton.)

Figure 13: Henry Cotton collection, Spring/Summer 2015. (Photo by Henry Cotton.)

Figure 14: Henry Cotton collection. (Photo by Henry Cotton.)

Figure 15: Eataly Expo 2015 in Milan, Italy. (Photo by Henry Cotton.)

with classic silhouettes. Due to his impeccable golf record, he became one of the first sports icons to attain sponsorship deals. One of his most noteworthy deals was with Dunlop Balls, which developed the Dunlop 65 Collection that remains in production today. Cotton also acquired deals with Lotus for footwear and Brooks Brothers for casual clothing. Following his immense success, he partnered with mills and production facilities in Italy to develop men's clothing and accessories. He is famous for saying, 'When it comes to clothes, I believe in Quality'.

The brand has been featured in *Vanity Fair* and recognized for its innovative visual strategy that highlights an array of material selections, colour palettes and eye-catching window displays. The most recent collection implements lush gardens, safari-style garments, and adds a juxtaposition of Adam and Eve in beautiful lush gardens.

One of the major attractions for Italy in 2015 was the Universal World Expo. Over 150 countries participated in a six-month exhibition demonstrating their resources to address healthy, safe and sufficient food for the people on the planet. Over 20 million visitors explored the innovative pavilions and engaged in dialogue, which focused on the central theme, 'Feeding the Planet Energy for Life'. Trend forecasting companies from all over the world flocked to the World Expo to search for ideas to incorporate into their own lines, especially if the brand's strategy implemented elements of sustainability.

References

Berg (2016), *Berg Fashion Library*, http://www.bergfashionlibrary. com/start;jsessionid=C6C872B639B2B192A89DFEFD-389FE402?authRejection=true&url=/view/FASHWRLDCIT/ chapter-FASHWRLDCIT0007.xml. Accessed 3 June 2015.

Breward, Christopher (2006), 'Fashion Cities', *Berg Fashion Library*, http://www.bergfashionlibrary.com/view/bewdf/BEWDF-v10/ EDch10030.xml. Accessed 3 June 2015.

Cotton Incorporated (2015), https://www.thefabricofourlives.com/ common-threads/trendcasters. Accessed 26 March 2015.

Gilbert, David (2011), 'From Paris to Shanghai: The Changing Geographies of Fashion's World Cities', in Christopher Breward and David Gilbert (eds), *Fashion's World Cities*, Oxford: Berg, pp. 3-32.

Jackson, Peter, Crang, Philip and Dwyer, Claire (2004), *Transnational Spaces*, New York: Routledge, Taylor & Francis Group.

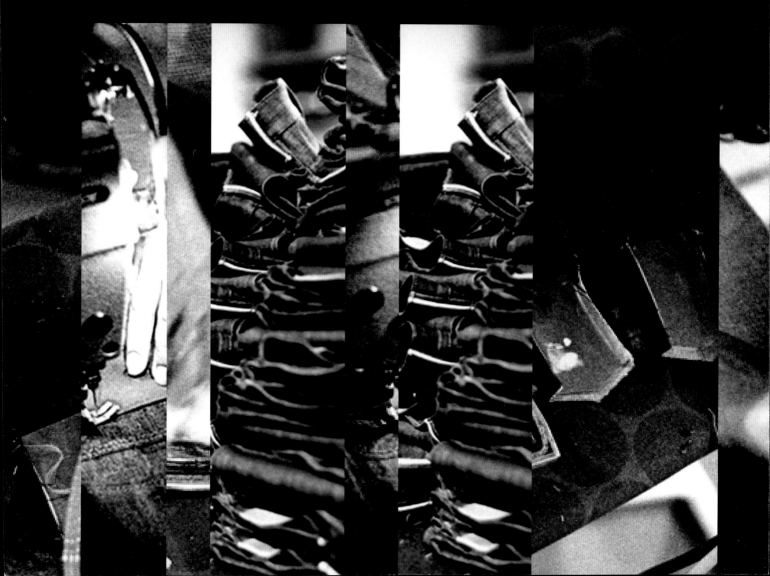

Stevie Guarino graduated from Drexel University in the Custom-Design Major program. She worked under the guidance of Dr. Hancock to produce a program that allowed her to examine retail entrepreneurship. Her final project was based upon her chapter Raleigh Denim.

Joseph H. Hancock, II, Ph.D., is a Professor at Drexel University. He comes from a twenty-year retailing background having worked for Gap Inc., The Limited Brands, and at Target Corporation. He is an international authority in the area of fashion branding as a form of storytelling. He just released the 2nd Edition of his book *Brand/Story: Explorations and Cases in Fashion Branding* (Bloomsbury 2016). His works on branding and storytelling have appeared in such publications as *The Brand Challenge* by Kartikeya Kompella (Kogan Page 2016) and *Strategic Design Thinking* by Natalie Nixon (Bloomsbury 2015). Dr. Hancock is the principal editor of the peer-reviewed and indexed journal *Fashion, Style and Popular Culture* (Intellect Ltd).

Shahidah Hasan is a graduate student in the Kanbar College of Design, Engineering & Commerce. Shahidah is studying the business of fashion in the Global Fashion Enterprise programme. Shahidah is currently Assistant Buyer at Burlington Stores, Inc.

Nissa Lee teaches in the English departments at Rowan University and Rutgers University-Camden, where she earned her BA in English and MFA in Creative Writing, respectively. Her poetry is published in *Stirring: A Literary Collection*, *Mason's Road*, *The Raleigh Review*, *Philadelphia Stories*, and elsewhere.

Tasha L. Lewis, Ph.D., is Assistant Professor in the Department of Fiber Science & Apparel Design at Cornell University where she teaches in the area of fashion design management. Her research interests include the disruptive impact of technology in the apparel industry, the behaviour of fashion brands, global and domestic apparel production ('glocalization') issues, and the significance of social responsibility and sustainability throughout the apparel supply chain. Dr Lewis has also worked in the apparel industry in areas of production, sourcing and retail operations and maintains ongoing contact with industry professionals to inform her research. She is a faculty fellow of Cornell's Atkinson Center for a Sustainable Future and a research fellow in the Innovation & Entrepreneurship Research Initiative housed in Cornell's Charles H. Dyson School of Applied Economics. Dr Lewis also serves as a member of the editorial board for the journal *Fashion, Style and Popular Culture* (Intellect Ltd).

Autumn S. Newell studied fashion design at the Fashion Institute of Technology in New York City and has a BS in business and managerial economics from SUNY Empire State College. She also earned an MA from the Department of Fiber Science and Apparel Design at Cornell University, where she researched textile recycling systems. Prior to her graduate studies at Cornell, she owned and operated an eco-fashion retail boutique and ran a fashion design apprentice programme for youth that cultivated environmental stewardship and career exploration through teens' interest in fashion.

Sarah Portway has ten years of fashion industry experience as both a retailer and educator. She has earned a Master's degree in fashion from Ryerson University and a Bachelor's degree in studio art from the University of Guelph. Portway has also been honoured with several prestigious awards, notably including a current doctoral fellowship from the Social Sciences and Humanities Research Council of Canada. Portway is undertaking her Ph.D. in apparel design at Cornell University and expects to graduate in 2018.

Virginia Theerman is a Drexel University undergraduate dual majoring in design and merchandising and art history. For the past three years she has worked in the Robert and Penny Fox Historic Costume Collection at Drexel, and intends to further pursue her passion for costume history in a Master's or Ph.D. programme after graduation. She fully blames her mother, historic preservationist and vintage shopper, and her father, archivist and academic extraordinaire, for getting her into this mess.

Helen Trejo is a Ph.D. student in fibre science and apparel design at Cornell University. Her current research focuses on exploring the farm-to-fashion supply chain with small farms and fibre-producing animals such as sheep, alpacas and angora goats in New York State. She completed her MA at Cornell University in 2014. She attended the University of California, Davis and received her BA in fashion design with a minor in textiles and clothing in 2012.

Nioka N. Wyatt is an associate professor in the fashion merchandising and management programme at Philadelphia University. Nioka spent her tenure working at QVC in the quality assurance department and later transitioned into jewellery production for a number of celebrities. Nioka is a consultant in the areas of product development, omni-channel retailing, and travels extensively to conduct research in China. She teaches graduate and undergraduate courses in design thinking and fashion business development, and she conducts a course to China to provide experiential learning opportunities for fashion students. Nioka's most recent project involved students developing product extensions for Isaac Mizrahi and Halston.